Twelve Stories a

H. G. Wells

Alpha Editions

This edition published in 2024

ISBN : 9789362519993

Design and Setting By
Alpha Editions
www.alphaedis.com
Email - info@alphaedis.com

As per information held with us this book is in Public Domain.
This book is a reproduction of an important historical work. Alpha Editions uses the best technology to reproduce historical work in the same manner it was first published to preserve its original nature. Any marks or number seen are left intentionally to preserve its true form.

Contents

1. FILMER ....- 1 -
2. THE MAGIC SHOP ....- 15 -
3. THE VALLEY OF SPIDERS ....- 25 -
4. THE TRUTH ABOUT PYECRAFT ....- 35 -
5. MR. SKELMERSDALE IN FAIRYLAND ....- 45 -
6. THE STORY OF THE INEXPERIENCED GHOST ....- 56 -
7. JIMMY GOGGLES THE GOD ....- 68 -
8. THE NEW ACCELERATOR ....- 78 -
9. MR. LEDBETTER'S VACATION ....- 90 -
10. THE STOLEN BODY ....- 105 -
11. MR. BRISHER'S TREASURE ....- 118 -
12. MISS WINCHELSEA'S HEART ....- 127 -
13. A DREAM OF ARMAGEDDON ....- 141 -

1. FILMER

In truth the mastery of flying was the work of thousands of men—this man a suggestion and that an experiment, until at last only one vigorous intellectual effort was needed to finish the work. But the inexorable injustice of the popular mind has decided that of all these thousands, one man, and that a man who never flew, should be chosen as the discoverer, just as it has chosen to honour Watt as the discoverer of steam and Stephenson of the steam-engine. And surely of all honoured names none is so grotesquely and tragically honoured as poor Filmer's, the timid, intellectual creature who solved the problem over which the world had hung perplexed and a little fearful for so many generations, the man who pressed the button that has changed peace and warfare and well-nigh every condition of human life and happiness. Never has that recurring wonder of the littleness of the scientific man in the face of the greatness of his science found such an amazing exemplification. Much concerning Filmer is, and must remain, profoundly obscure—Filmers attract no Boswells—but the essential facts and the concluding scene are clear enough, and there are letters, and notes, and casual allusions to piece the whole together. And this is the story one makes, putting this thing with that, of Filmer's life and death.

The first authentic trace of Filmer on the page of history is a document in which he applies for admission as a paid student in physics to the Government laboratories at South Kensington, and therein he describes himself as the son of a "military bootmaker" ("cobbler" in the vulgar tongue) of Dover, and lists his various examination proofs of a high proficiency in chemistry and mathematics. With a certain want of dignity he seeks to enhance these attainments by a profession of poverty and disadvantages, and he writes of the laboratory as the "gaol" of his ambitions, a slip which reinforces his claim to have devoted himself exclusively to the exact sciences. The document is endorsed in a manner that shows Filmer was admitted to this coveted opportunity; but until quite recently no traces of his success in the Government institution could be found.

It has now, however, been shown that in spite of his professed zeal for research, Filmer, before he had held this scholarship a year, was tempted, by the possibility of a small increase in his immediate income, to abandon it in order to become one of the nine-pence-an-hour computers employed by a well-known Professor in his vicarious conduct of those extensive researches of his in solar physics—researches which are still a matter of perplexity to astronomers. Afterwards, for the space of seven years, save for the pass lists of the London University, in which he is seen to climb slowly to a double first class B.Sc., in mathematics and chemistry, there is no evidence of how

Filmer passed his life. No one knows how or where he lived, though it seems highly probable that he continued to support himself by teaching while he prosecuted the studies necessary for this distinction. And then, oddly enough, one finds him mentioned in the correspondence of Arthur Hicks, the poet.

"You remember Filmer," Hicks writes to his friend Vance; "well, HE hasn't altered a bit, the same hostile mumble and the nasty chin—how CAN a man contrive to be always three days from shaving?—and a sort of furtive air of being engaged in sneaking in front of one; even his coat and that frayed collar of his show no further signs of the passing years. He was writing in the library and I sat down beside him in the name of God's charity, whereupon he deliberately insulted me by covering up his memoranda. It seems he has some brilliant research on hand that he suspects me of all people—with a Bodley Booklet a-printing!—of stealing. He has taken remarkable honours at the University—he went through them with a sort of hasty slobber, as though he feared I might interrupt him before he had told me all—and he spoke of taking his D.Sc. as one might speak of taking a cab. And he asked what I was doing—with a sort of comparative accent, and his arm was spread nervously, positively a protecting arm, over the paper that hid the precious idea—his one hopeful idea.

"'Poetry,' he said, 'Poetry. And what do you profess to teach in it, Hicks?'

"The thing's a Provincial professorling in the very act of budding, and I thank the Lord devoutly that but for the precious gift of indolence I also might have gone this way to D.Sc. and destruction..."

A curious little vignette that I am inclined to think caught Filmer in or near the very birth of his discovery. Hicks was wrong in anticipating a provincial professorship for Filmer. Our next glimpse of him is lecturing on "rubber and rubber substitutes," to the Society of Arts—he had become manager to a great plastic-substance manufactory—and at that time, it is now known, he was a member of the Aeronautical Society, albeit he contributed nothing to the discussions of that body, preferring no doubt to mature his great conception without external assistance. And within two years of that paper before the Society of Arts he was hastily taking out a number of patents and proclaiming in various undignified ways the completion of the divergent inquiries which made his flying machine possible. The first definite statement to that effect appeared in a halfpenny evening paper through the agency of a man who lodged in the same house with Filmer. His final haste after his long laborious secret patience seems to have been due to a needless panic, Bootle, the notorious American scientific quack, having made an announcement that Filmer interpreted wrongly as an anticipation of his idea.

Now what precisely was Filmer's idea? Really a very simple one. Before his time the pursuit of aeronautics had taken two divergent lines, and had developed on the one hand balloons—large apparatus lighter than air, easy in ascent, and comparatively safe in descent, but floating helplessly before any breeze that took them; and on the other, flying machines that flew only in theory—vast flat structures heavier than air, propelled and kept up by heavy engines and for the most part smashing at the first descent. But, neglecting the fact that the inevitable final collapse rendered them impossible, the weight of the flying machines gave them this theoretical advantage, that they could go through the air against a wind, a necessary condition if aerial navigation was to have any practical value. It is Filmer's particular merit that he perceived the way in which the contrasted and hitherto incompatible merits of balloon and heavy flying machine might be combined in one apparatus, which should be at choice either heavier or lighter than air. He took hints from the contractile bladders of fish and the pneumatic cavities of birds. He devised an arrangement of contractile and absolutely closed balloons which when expanded could lift the actual flying apparatus with ease, and when retracted by the complicated "musculature" he wove about them, were withdrawn almost completely into the frame; and he built the large framework which these balloons sustained, of hollow, rigid tubes, the air in which, by an ingenious contrivance, was automatically pumped out as the apparatus fell, and which then remained exhausted so long as the aeronaut desired. There were no wings or propellers to his machine, such as there had been to all previous aeroplanes, and the only engine required was the compact and powerful little appliance needed to contract the balloons. He perceived that such an apparatus as he had devised might rise with frame exhausted and balloons expanded to a considerable height, might then contract its balloons and let the air into its frame, and by an adjustment of its weights slide down the air in any desired direction. As it fell it would accumulate velocity and at the same time lose weight, and the momentum accumulated by its down-rush could be utilised by means of a shifting of its weights to drive it up in the air again as the balloons expanded. This conception, which is still the structural conception of all successful flying machines, needed, however, a vast amount of toil upon its details before it could actually be realised, and such toil Filmer—as he was accustomed to tell the numerous interviewers who crowded upon him in the heyday of his fame—"ungrudgingly and unsparingly gave." His particular difficulty was the elastic lining of the contractile balloon. He found he needed a new substance, and in the discovery and manufacture of that new substance he had, as he never failed to impress upon the interviewers, "performed a far more arduous work than even in the actual achievement of my seemingly greater discovery."

But it must not be imagined that these interviews followed hard upon Filmer's proclamation of his invention. An interval of nearly five years elapsed during which he timidly remained at his rubber factory—he seems to have been entirely dependent on his small income from this source—making misdirected attempts to assure a quite indifferent public that he really HAD invented what he had invented. He occupied the greater part of his leisure in the composition of letters to the scientific and daily press, and so forth, stating precisely the net result of his contrivances, and demanding financial aid. That alone would have sufficed for the suppression of his letters. He spent such holidays as he could arrange in unsatisfactory interviews with the door-keepers of leading London papers—he was singularly not adapted for inspiring hall-porters with confidence—and he positively attempted to induce the War Office to take up his work with him. There remains a confidential letter from Major-General Volleyfire to the Earl of Frogs. "The man's a crank and a bounder to boot," says the Major-General in his bluff, sensible, army way, and so left it open for the Japanese to secure, as they subsequently did, the priority in this side of warfare—a priority they still to our great discomfort retain.

And then by a stroke of luck the membrane Filmer had invented for his contractile balloon was discovered to be useful for the valves of a new oil-engine, and he obtained the means for making a trial model of his invention. He threw up his rubber factory appointment, desisted from all further writing, and, with a certain secrecy that seems to have been an inseparable characteristic of all his proceedings, set to work upon the apparatus. He seems to have directed the making of its parts and collected most of it in a room in Shoreditch, but its final putting together was done at Dymchurch, in Kent. He did not make the affair large enough to carry a man, but he made an extremely ingenious use of what were then called the Marconi rays to control its flight. The first flight of this first practicable flying machine took place over some fields near Burford Bridge, near Hythe, in Kent, and Filmer followed and controlled its flight upon a specially constructed motor tricycle.

The flight was, considering all things, an amazing success. The apparatus was brought in a cart from Dymchurch to Burford Bridge, ascended there to a height of nearly three hundred feet, swooped thence very nearly back to Dymchurch, came about in its sweep, rose again, circled, and finally sank uninjured in a field behind the Burford Bridge Inn. At its descent a curious thing happened. Filmer got off his tricycle, scrambled over the intervening dyke, advanced perhaps twenty yards towards his triumph, threw out his arms in a strange gesticulation, and fell down in a dead faint. Every one could then recall the ghastliness of his features and all the evidences of extreme excitement they had observed throughout the trial, things they might otherwise have forgotten. Afterwards in the inn he had an unaccountable gust of hysterical weeping.

Altogether there were not twenty witnesses of this affair, and those for the most part uneducated men. The New Romney doctor saw the ascent but not the descent, his horse being frightened by the electrical apparatus on Filmer's tricycle and giving him a nasty spill. Two members of the Kent constabulary watched the affair from a cart in an unofficial spirit, and a grocer calling round the Marsh for orders and two lady cyclists seem almost to complete the list of educated people. There were two reporters present, one representing a Folkestone paper and the other being a fourth-class interviewer and "symposium" journalist, whose expenses down, Filmer, anxious as ever for adequate advertisement—and now quite realising the way in which adequate advertisement may be obtained—had paid. The latter was one of those writers who can throw a convincing air of unreality over the most credible events, and his half-facetious account of the affair appeared in the magazine page of a popular journal. But, happily for Filmer, this person's colloquial methods were more convincing. He went to offer some further screed upon the subject to Banghurst, the proprietor of the New Paper, and one of the ablest and most unscrupulous men in London journalism, and Banghurst instantly seized upon the situation. The interviewer vanishes from the narrative, no doubt very doubtfully remunerated, and Banghurst, Banghurst himself, double chin, grey twill suit, abdomen, voice, gestures and all, appears at Dymchurch, following his large, unrivalled journalistic nose. He had seen the whole thing at a glance, just what it was and what it might be.

At his touch, as it were, Filmer's long-pent investigations exploded into fame. He instantly and most magnificently was a Boom. One turns over the files of the journals of the year 1907 with a quite incredulous recognition of how swift and flaming the boom of those days could be. The July papers know nothing of flying, see nothing in flying, state by a most effective silence that men never would, could or should fly. In August flying and Filmer and flying and parachutes and aerial tactics and the Japanese Government and Filmer and again flying, shouldered the war in Yunnan and the gold mines of Upper Greenland off the leading page. And Banghurst had given ten thousand pounds, and, further, Banghurst was giving five thousand pounds, and Banghurst had devoted his well-known, magnificent (but hitherto sterile) private laboratories and several acres of land near his private residence on the Surrey hills to the strenuous and violent completion—Banghurst fashion—of the life-size practicable flying machine. Meanwhile, in the sight of privileged multitudes in the walled-garden of the Banghurst town residence in Fulham, Filmer was exhibited at weekly garden parties putting the working model through its paces. At enormous initial cost, but with a final profit, the New Paper presented its readers with a beautiful photographic souvenir of the first of these occasions.

Here again the correspondence of Arthur Hicks and his friend Vance comes to our aid.

"I saw Filmer in his glory," he writes, with just the touch of envy natural to his position as a poet passe. "The man is brushed and shaved, dressed in the fashion of a Royal-Institution-Afternoon Lecturer, the very newest shape in frock-coats and long patent shoes, and altogether in a state of extraordinary streakiness between an owlish great man and a scared abashed self-conscious bounder cruelly exposed. He hasn't a touch of colour in the skin of his face, his head juts forward, and those queer little dark amber eyes of his watch furtively round him for his fame. His clothes fit perfectly and yet sit upon him as though he had bought them ready-made. He speaks in a mumble still, but he says, you perceive indistinctly, enormous self-assertive things, he backs into the rear of groups by instinct if Banghurst drops the line for a minute, and when he walks across Banghurst's lawn one perceives him a little out of breath and going jerky, and that his weak white hands are clenched. His is a state of tension—horrible tension. And he is the Greatest Discoverer of This or Any Age—the Greatest Discoverer of This or Any Age! What strikes one so forcibly about him is that he didn't somehow quite expect it ever, at any rate, not at all like this. Banghurst is about everywhere, the energetic M.C. of his great little catch, and I swear he will have every one down on his lawn there before he has finished with the engine; he had bagged the prime minister yesterday, and he, bless his heart! didn't look particularly outsize, on the very first occasion. Conceive it! Filmer! Our obscure unwashed Filmer, the Glory of British science! Duchesses crowd upon him, beautiful, bold peeresses say in their beautiful, clear loud voices—have you noticed how penetrating the great lady is becoming nowadays?—'Oh, Mr. Filmer, how DID you do it?'

"Common men on the edge of things are too remote for the answer. One imagines something in the way of that interview, 'toil ungrudgingly and unsparingly given, Madam, and, perhaps—I don't know—but perhaps a little special aptitude.'"

So far Hicks, and the photographic supplement to the New Paper is in sufficient harmony with the description. In one picture the machine swings down towards the river, and the tower of Fulham church appears below it through a gap in the elms, and in another, Filmer sits at his guiding batteries, and the great and beautiful of the earth stand around him, with Banghurst massed modestly but resolutely in the rear. The grouping is oddly apposite. Occluding much of Banghurst, and looking with a pensive, speculative expression at Filmer, stands the Lady Mary Elkinghorn, still beautiful, in spite of the breath of scandal and her eight-and-thirty years, the only person whose face does not admit a perception of the camera that was in the act of snapping them all.

So much for the exterior facts of the story, but, after all, they are very exterior facts. About the real interest of the business one is necessarily very much in the dark. How was Filmer feeling at the time? How much was a certain unpleasant anticipation present inside that very new and fashionable frock-coat? He was in the halfpenny, penny, six-penny, and more expensive papers alike, and acknowledged by the whole world as "the Greatest Discoverer of This or Any Age." He had invented a practicable flying machine, and every day down among the Surrey hills the life-sized model was getting ready. And when it was ready, it followed as a clear inevitable consequence of his having invented and made it—everybody in the world, indeed, seemed to take it for granted; there wasn't a gap anywhere in that serried front of anticipation—that he would proudly and cheerfully get aboard it, ascend with it, and fly.

But we know now pretty clearly that simple pride and cheerfulness in such an act were singularly out of harmony with Filmer's private constitution. It occurred to no one at the time, but there the fact is. We can guess with some confidence now that it must have been drifting about in his mind a great deal during the day, and, from a little note to his physician complaining of persistent insomnia, we have the soundest reason for supposing it dominated his nights,—the idea that it would be after all, in spite of his theoretical security, an abominably sickening, uncomfortable, and dangerous thing for him to flap about in nothingness a thousand feet or so in the air. It must have dawned upon him quite early in the period of being the Greatest Discoverer of This or Any Age, the vision of doing this and that with an extensive void below. Perhaps somewhen in his youth he had looked down a great height or fallen down in some excessively uncomfortable way; perhaps some habit of sleeping on the wrong side had resulted in that disagreeable falling nightmare one knows, and given him his horror; of the strength of that horror there remains now not a particle of doubt.

Apparently he had never weighed this duty of flying in his earlier days of research; the machine had been his end, but now things were opening out beyond his end, and particularly this giddy whirl up above there. He was a Discoverer and he had Discovered. But he was not a Flying Man, and it was only now that he was beginning to perceive clearly that he was expected to fly. Yet, however much the thing was present in his mind he gave no expression to it until the very end, and meanwhile he went to and fro from Banghurst's magnificent laboratories, and was interviewed and lionised, and wore good clothes, and ate good food, and lived in an elegant flat, enjoying a very abundant feast of such good, coarse, wholesome Fame and Success as a man, starved for all his years as he had been starved, might be reasonably expected to enjoy.

After a time, the weekly gatherings in Fulham ceased. The model had failed one day just for a moment to respond to Filmer's guidance, or he had been distracted by the compliments of an archbishop. At any rate, it suddenly dug its nose into the air just a little too steeply as the archbishop was sailing through a Latin quotation for all the world like an archbishop in a book, and it came down in the Fulham Road within three yards of a 'bus horse. It stood for a second perhaps, astonishing and in its attitude astonished, then it crumpled, shivered into pieces, and the 'bus horse was incidentally killed.

Filmer lost the end of the archiepiscopal compliment. He stood up and stared as his invention swooped out of sight and reach of him. His long, white hands still gripped his useless apparatus. The archbishop followed his skyward stare with an apprehension unbecoming in an archbishop.

Then came the crash and the shouts and uproar from the road to relieve Filmer's tension. "My God!" he whispered, and sat down.

Every one else almost was staring to see where the machine had vanished, or rushing into the house.

The making of the big machine progressed all the more rapidly for this. Over its making presided Filmer, always a little slow and very careful in his manner, always with a growing preoccupation in his mind. His care over the strength and soundness of the apparatus was prodigious. The slightest doubt, and he delayed everything until the doubtful part could be replaced. Wilkinson, his senior assistant, fumed at some of these delays, which, he insisted, were for the most part unnecessary. Banghurst magnified the patient certitude of Filmer in the New Paper, and reviled it bitterly to his wife, and MacAndrew, the second assistant, approved Filmer's wisdom. "We're not wanting a fiasco, man," said MacAndrew. "He's perfectly well advised."

And whenever an opportunity arose Filmer would expound to Wilkinson and MacAndrew just exactly how every part of the flying machine was to be controlled and worked, so that in effect they would be just as capable, and even more capable, when at last the time came, of guiding it through the skies.

Now I should imagine that if Filmer had seen fit at this stage to define just what he was feeling, and to take a definite line in the matter of his ascent, he might have escaped that painful ordeal quite easily. If he had had it clearly in his mind he could have done endless things. He would surely have found no difficulty with a specialist to demonstrate a weak heart, or something gastric or pulmonary, to stand in his way—that is the line I am astonished he did not take,—or he might, had he been man enough, have declared simply and finally that he did not intend to do the thing. But the fact is, though the dread was hugely present in his mind, the thing was by no means sharp and clear. I fancy that all through this period he kept telling himself that when the occasion came he would find himself equal to it. He was like a man just gripped by a great illness, who says he feels a little out of sorts, and expects to be better presently. Meanwhile he delayed the completion of the machine, and let the assumption that he was going to fly it take root and flourish exceedingly about him. He even accepted anticipatory compliments on his courage. And, barring this secret squeamishness, there can be no doubt he found all the praise and distinction and fuss he got a delightful and even intoxicating draught.

The Lady Mary Elkinghorn made things a little more complicated for him.

How THAT began was a subject of inexhaustible speculation to Hicks. Probably in the beginning she was just a little "nice" to him with that impartial partiality of hers, and it may be that to her eyes, standing out conspicuously as he did ruling his monster in the upper air, he had a distinction that Hicks was not disposed to find. And somehow they must have had a moment of sufficient isolation, and the great Discoverer a moment of sufficient courage for something just a little personal to be mumbled or blurted. However it began, there is no doubt that it did begin, and presently became quite perceptible to a world accustomed to find in the proceedings of the Lady Mary Elkinghorn a matter of entertainment. It complicated things, because the state of love in such a virgin mind as Filmer's would brace his resolution, if not sufficiently, at any rate considerably towards facing a danger he feared, and hampered him in such attempts at evasion as would otherwise be natural and congenial.

It remains a matter for speculation just how the Lady Mary felt for Filmer and just what she thought of him. At thirty-eight one may have gathered much wisdom and still be not altogether wise, and the imagination still functions actively enough in creating glamours and effecting the impossible. He came before her eyes as a very central man, and that always counts, and he had powers, unique powers as it seemed, at any rate in the air. The performance with the model had just a touch of the quality of a potent incantation, and women have ever displayed an unreasonable disposition to imagine that when a man has powers he must necessarily have Power. Given so much, and what was not good in Filmer's manner and appearance became an added merit. He was modest, he hated display, but given an occasion where TRUE qualities are needed, then—then one would see!

The late Mrs. Bampton thought it wise to convey to Lady Mary her opinion that Filmer, all things considered, was rather a "grub." "He's certainly not a sort of man I have ever met before," said the Lady Mary, with a quite unruffled serenity. And Mrs. Bampton, after a swift, imperceptible glance at that serenity, decided that so far as saying anything to Lady Mary went, she had done as much as could be expected of her. But she said a great deal to other people.

And at last, without any undue haste or unseemliness, the day dawned, the great day, when Banghurst had promised his public—the world in fact—that flying should be finally attained and overcome. Filmer saw it dawn, watched even in the darkness before it dawned, watched its stars fade and the grey and pearly pinks give place at last to the clear blue sky of a sunny, cloudless day. He watched it from the window of his bedroom in the new-built wing of Banghurst's Tudor house. And as the stars were overwhelmed and the shapes and substances of things grew into being out of the amorphous dark, he must have seen more and more distinctly the festive preparations beyond the beech clumps near the green pavilion in the outer park, the three stands for the privileged spectators, the raw, new fencing of the enclosure, the sheds and workshops, the Venetian masts and fluttering flags that Banghurst had considered essential, black and limp in the breezeless dawn, and amidst all these things a great shape covered with tarpauling. A strange and terrible portent for humanity was that shape, a beginning that must surely spread and widen and change and dominate all the affairs of men, but to Filmer it is very doubtful whether it appeared in anything but a narrow and personal light. Several people heard him pacing in the small hours—for the vast place was packed with guests by a proprietor editor who, before all understood compression. And about five o'clock, if not before, Filmer left his room and wandered out of the sleeping house into the park, alive by that time with sunlight and birds and squirrels and the fallow deer. MacAndrew, who was also an early riser, met him near the machine, and they went and had a look at it together.

It is doubtful if Filmer took any breakfast, in spite of the urgency of Banghurst. So soon as the guests began to be about in some number he seems to have retreated to his room. Thence about ten he went into the shrubbery, very probably because he had seen the Lady Mary Elkinghorn there. She was walking up and down, engaged in conversation with her old school friend, Mrs. Brewis-Craven, and although Filmer had never met the latter lady before, he joined them and walked beside them for some time. There were several silences in spite of the Lady Mary's brilliance. The situation was a difficult one, and Mrs. Brewis-Craven did not master its difficulty. "He struck me," she said afterwards with a luminous self-contradiction, "as a very unhappy person who had something to say, and wanted before all things to be helped to say it. But how was one to help him when one didn't know what it was?"

At half-past eleven the enclosures for the public in the outer park were crammed, there was an intermittent stream of equipages along the belt which circles the outer park, and the house party was dotted over the lawn and shrubbery and the corner of the inner park, in a series of brilliantly attired knots, all making for the flying machine. Filmer walked in a group of three with Banghurst, who was supremely and conspicuously happy, and Sir Theodore Hickle, the president of the Aeronautical Society. Mrs. Banghurst was close behind with the Lady Mary Elkinghorn, Georgina Hickle, and the Dean of Stays. Banghurst was large and copious in speech, and such interstices as he left were filled in by Hickle with complimentary remarks to Filmer. And Filmer walked between them saying not a word except by way of unavoidable reply. Behind, Mrs. Banghurst listened to the admirably suitable and shapely conversation of the Dean with that fluttered attention to the ampler clergy ten years of social ascent and ascendency had not cured in her; and the Lady Mary watched, no doubt with an entire confidence in the world's disillusionment, the drooping shoulders of the sort of man she had never met before.

There was some cheering as the central party came into view of the enclosures, but it was not very unanimous nor invigorating cheering. They were within fifty yards of the apparatus when Filmer took a hasty glance over his shoulder to measure the distance of the ladies behind them, and decided to make the first remark he had initiated since the house had been left. His voice was just a little hoarse, and he cut in on Banghurst in mid-sentence on Progress.

"I say, Banghurst," he said, and stopped.

"Yes," said Banghurst.

"I wish—" He moistened his lips. "I'm not feeling well."

Banghurst stopped dead. "Eh?" he shouted.

"A queer feeling." Filmer made to move on, but Banghurst was immovable. "I don't know. I may be better in a minute. If not—perhaps... MacAndrew—"

"You're not feeling WELL?" said Banghurst, and stared at his white face.

"My dear!" he said, as Mrs. Banghurst came up with them, "Filmer says he isn't feeling WELL."

"A little queer," exclaimed Filmer, avoiding the Lady Mary's eyes. "It may pass off—"

There was a pause.

It came to Filmer that he was the most isolated person in the world.

"In any case," said Banghurst, "the ascent must be made. Perhaps if you were to sit down somewhere for a moment—"

"It's the crowd, I think," said Filmer.

There was a second pause. Banghurst's eye rested in scrutiny on Filmer, and then swept the sample of public in the enclosure.

"It's unfortunate," said Sir Theodore Hickle; "but still—I suppose—Your assistants—Of course, if you feel out of condition and disinclined—"

"I don't think Mr. Filmer would permit THAT for a moment," said Lady Mary.

"But if Mr. Filmer's nerve is run—It might even be dangerous for him to attempt—" Hickle coughed.

"It's just because it's dangerous," began the Lady Mary, and felt she had made her point of view and Filmer's plain enough.

Conflicting motives struggled for Filmer.

"I feel I ought to go up," he said, regarding the ground. He looked up and met the Lady Mary's eyes. "I want to go up," he said, and smiled whitely at her. He turned towards Banghurst. "If I could just sit down somewhere for a moment out of the crowd and sun—"

Banghurst, at least, was beginning to understand the case. "Come into my little room in the green pavilion," he said. "It's quite cool there." He took Filmer by the arm.

Filmer turned his face to the Lady Mary Elkinghorn again. "I shall be all right in five minutes," he said. "I'm tremendously sorry—"

The Lady Mary Elkinghorn smiled at him. "I couldn't think—" he said to Hickle, and obeyed the compulsion of Banghurst's pull.

The rest remained watching the two recede.

"He is so fragile," said the Lady Mary.

"He's certainly a highly nervous type," said the Dean, whose weakness it was to regard the whole world, except married clergymen with enormous families, as "neurotic."

"Of course," said Hickle, "it isn't absolutely necessary for him to go up because he has invented—"

"How COULD he avoid it?" asked the Lady Mary, with the faintest shadow of scorn.

"It's certainly most unfortunate if he's going to be ill now," said Mrs. Banghurst a little severely.

"He's not going to be ill," said the Lady Mary, and certainly she had met Filmer's eye.

"YOU'LL be all right," said Banghurst, as they went towards the pavilion. "All you want is a nip of brandy. It ought to be you, you know. You'll be— you'd get it rough, you know, if you let another man—"

"Oh, I want to go," said Filmer. "I shall be all right. As a matter of fact I'm almost inclined NOW—. No! I think I'll have that nip of brandy first."

Banghurst took him into the little room and routed out an empty decanter. He departed in search of a supply. He was gone perhaps five minutes.

The history of those five minutes cannot be written. At intervals Filmer's face could be seen by the people on the easternmost of the stands erected for spectators, against the window pane peering out, and then it would recede and fade. Banghurst vanished shouting behind the grand stand, and presently the butler appeared going pavilionward with a tray.

The apartment in which Filmer came to his last solution was a pleasant little room very simply furnished with green furniture and an old bureau—for Banghurst was simple in all his private ways. It was hung with little engravings after Morland and it had a shelf of books. But as it happened, Banghurst had left a rook rifle he sometimes played with on the top of the desk, and on the corner of the mantelshelf was a tin with three or four cartridges remaining in it. As Filmer went up and down that room wrestling with his intolerable dilemma he went first towards the neat little rifle athwart the blotting-pad and then towards the neat little red label

".22 LONG."

The thing must have jumped into his mind in a moment.

Nobody seems to have connected the report with him, though the gun, being fired in a confined space, must have sounded loud, and there were several people in the billiard-room, separated from him only by a lath-and-plaster partition. But directly Banghurst's butler opened the door and smelt the sour smell of the smoke, he knew, he says, what had happened. For the servants at least of Banghurst's household had guessed something of what was going on in Filmer's mind.

All through that trying afternoon Banghurst behaved as he held a man should behave in the presence of hopeless disaster, and his guests for the most part succeeded in not insisting upon the fact—though to conceal their perception of it altogether was impossible—that Banghurst had been pretty elaborately and completely swindled by the deceased. The public in the enclosure, Hicks told me, dispersed "like a party that has been ducking a welsher," and there wasn't a soul in the train to London, it seems, who hadn't known all along that flying was a quite impossible thing for man. "But he might have tried it," said many, "after carrying the thing so far."

In the evening, when he was comparatively alone, Banghurst broke down and went on like a man of clay. I have been told he wept, which must have made an imposing scene, and he certainly said Filmer had ruined his life, and offered and sold the whole apparatus to MacAndrew for half-a-crown. "I've been thinking—" said MacAndrew at the conclusion of the bargain, and stopped.

The next morning the name of Filmer was, for the first time, less conspicuous in the New Paper than in any other daily paper in the world. The rest of the world's instructors, with varying emphasis, according to their dignity and the degree of competition between themselves and the New Paper, proclaimed the "Entire Failure of the New Flying Machine," and "Suicide of the Impostor." But in the district of North Surrey the reception of the news was tempered by a perception of unusual aerial phenomena.

Overnight Wilkinson and MacAndrew had fallen into violent argument on the exact motives of their principal's rash act.

"The man was certainly a poor, cowardly body, but so far as his science went he was NO impostor," said MacAndrew, "and I'm prepared to give that proposition a very practical demonstration, Mr. Wilkinson, so soon as we've got the place a little more to ourselves. For I've no faith in all this publicity for experimental trials."

And to that end, while all the world was reading of the certain failure of the new flying machine, MacAndrew was soaring and curvetting with great amplitude and dignity over the Epsom and Wimbledon divisions; and Banghurst, restored once more to hope and energy, and regardless of public security and the Board of Trade, was pursuing his gyrations and trying to attract his attention, on a motor car and in his pyjamas—he had caught sight of the ascent when pulling up the blind of his bedroom window—equipped, among other things, with a film camera that was subsequently discovered to be jammed. And Filmer was lying on the billiard table in the green pavilion with a sheet about his body.

2. THE MAGIC SHOP

I had seen the Magic Shop from afar several times; I had passed it once or twice, a shop window of alluring little objects, magic balls, magic hens, wonderful cones, ventriloquist dolls, the material of the basket trick, packs of cards that LOOKED all right, and all that sort of thing, but never had I thought of going in until one day, almost without warning, Gip hauled me by my finger right up to the window, and so conducted himself that there was nothing for it but to take him in. I had not thought the place was there, to tell the truth—a modest-sized frontage in Regent Street, between the picture shop and the place where the chicks run about just out of patent incubators, but there it was sure enough. I had fancied it was down nearer the Circus, or round the corner in Oxford Street, or even in Holborn; always over the way and a little inaccessible it had been, with something of the mirage in its position; but here it was now quite indisputably, and the fat end of Gip's pointing finger made a noise upon the glass.

"If I was rich," said Gip, dabbing a finger at the Disappearing Egg, "I'd buy myself that. And that"—which was The Crying Baby, Very Human—"and that," which was a mystery, and called, so a neat card asserted, "Buy One and Astonish Your Friends."

"Anything," said Gip, "will disappear under one of those cones. I have read about it in a book."

"And there, dadda, is the Vanishing Halfpenny—, only they've put it this way up so's we can't see how it's done."

Gip, dear boy, inherits his mother's breeding, and he did not propose to enter the shop or worry in any way; only, you know, quite unconsciously he lugged my finger doorward, and he made his interest clear.

"That," he said, and pointed to the Magic Bottle.

"If you had that?" I said; at which promising inquiry he looked up with a sudden radiance.

"I could show it to Jessie," he said, thoughtful as ever of others.

"It's less than a hundred days to your birthday, Gibbles," I said, and laid my hand on the door-handle.

Gip made no answer, but his grip tightened on my finger, and so we came into the shop.

It was no common shop this; it was a magic shop, and all the prancing precedence Gip would have taken in the matter of mere toys was wanting. He left the burthen of the conversation to me.

It was a little, narrow shop, not very well lit, and the door-bell pinged again with a plaintive note as we closed it behind us. For a moment or so we were alone and could glance about us. There was a tiger in papier-mache on the glass case that covered the low counter—a grave, kind-eyed tiger that waggled his head in a methodical manner; there were several crystal spheres, a china hand holding magic cards, a stock of magic fish-bowls in various sizes, and an immodest magic hat that shamelessly displayed its springs. On the floor were magic mirrors; one to draw you out long and thin, one to swell your head and vanish your legs, and one to make you short and fat like a draught; and while we were laughing at these the shopman, as I suppose, came in.

At any rate, there he was behind the counter—a curious, sallow, dark man, with one ear larger than the other and a chin like the toe-cap of a boot.

"What can we have the pleasure?" he said, spreading his long, magic fingers on the glass case; and so with a start we were aware of him.

"I want," I said, "to buy my little boy a few simple tricks."

"Legerdemain?" he asked. "Mechanical? Domestic?"

"Anything amusing?" said I.

"Um!" said the shopman, and scratched his head for a moment as if thinking. Then, quite distinctly, he drew from his head a glass ball. "Something in this way?" he said, and held it out.

The action was unexpected. I had seen the trick done at entertainments endless times before—it's part of the common stock of conjurers—but I had not expected it here.

"That's good," I said, with a laugh.

"Isn't it?" said the shopman.

Gip stretched out his disengaged hand to take this object and found merely a blank palm.

"It's in your pocket," said the shopman, and there it was!

"How much will that be?" I asked.

"We make no charge for glass balls," said the shopman politely. "We get them,"—he picked one out of his elbow as he spoke—"free." He produced another from the back of his neck, and laid it beside its predecessor on the counter. Gip regarded his glass ball sagely, then directed a look of inquiry at the two on the counter, and finally brought his round-eyed scrutiny to the shopman, who smiled.

"You may have those too," said the shopman, "and, if you DON'T mind, one from my mouth. SO!"

Gip counselled me mutely for a moment, and then in a profound silence put away the four balls, resumed my reassuring finger, and nerved himself for the next event.

"We get all our smaller tricks in that way," the shopman remarked.

I laughed in the manner of one who subscribes to a jest. "Instead of going to the wholesale shop," I said. "Of course, it's cheaper."

"In a way," the shopman said. "Though we pay in the end. But not so heavily—as people suppose.... Our larger tricks, and our daily provisions and all the other things we want, we get out of that hat... And you know, sir, if you'll excuse my saying it, there ISN'T a wholesale shop, not for Genuine Magic goods, sir. I don't know if you noticed our inscription—the Genuine Magic shop." He drew a business-card from his cheek and handed it to me. "Genuine," he said, with his finger on the word, and added, "There is absolutely no deception, sir."

He seemed to be carrying out the joke pretty thoroughly, I thought.

He turned to Gip with a smile of remarkable affability. "You, you know, are the Right Sort of Boy."

I was surprised at his knowing that, because, in the interests of discipline, we keep it rather a secret even at home; but Gip received it in unflinching silence, keeping a steadfast eye on him.

"It's only the Right Sort of Boy gets through that doorway."

And, as if by way of illustration, there came a rattling at the door, and a squeaking little voice could be faintly heard. "Nyar! I WARN 'a go in there, dadda, I WARN 'a go in there. Ny-a-a-ah!" and then the accents of a down-trodden parent, urging consolations and propitiations. "It's locked, Edward," he said.

"But it isn't," said I.

"It is, sir," said the shopman, "always—for that sort of child," and as he spoke we had a glimpse of the other youngster, a little, white face, pallid from sweet-eating and over-sapid food, and distorted by evil passions, a ruthless little egotist, pawing at the enchanted pane. "It's no good, sir," said the shopman, as I moved, with my natural helpfulness, doorward, and presently the spoilt child was carried off howling.

"How do you manage that?" I said, breathing a little more freely.

"Magic!" said the shopman, with a careless wave of the hand, and behold! sparks of coloured fire flew out of his fingers and vanished into the shadows of the shop.

"You were saying," he said, addressing himself to Gip, "before you came in, that you would like one of our 'Buy One and Astonish your Friends' boxes?"

Gip, after a gallant effort, said "Yes."

"It's in your pocket."

And leaning over the counter—he really had an extraordinarily long body—this amazing person produced the article in the customary conjurer's manner. "Paper," he said, and took a sheet out of the empty hat with the springs; "string," and behold his mouth was a string-box, from which he drew an unending thread, which when he had tied his parcel he bit off—and, it seemed to me, swallowed the ball of string. And then he lit a candle at the nose of one of the ventriloquist's dummies, stuck one of his fingers (which had become sealing-wax red) into the flame, and so sealed the parcel. "Then there was the Disappearing Egg," he remarked, and produced one from within my coat-breast and packed it, and also The Crying Baby, Very Human. I handed each parcel to Gip as it was ready, and he clasped them to his chest.

He said very little, but his eyes were eloquent; the clutch of his arms was eloquent. He was the playground of unspeakable emotions. These, you know, were REAL Magics. Then, with a start, I discovered something moving about in my hat—something soft and jumpy. I whipped it off, and a ruffled pigeon—no doubt a confederate—dropped out and ran on the counter, and went, I fancy, into a cardboard box behind the papier-mache tiger.

"Tut, tut!" said the shopman, dexterously relieving me of my headdress; "careless bird, and—as I live—nesting!"

He shook my hat, and shook out into his extended hand two or three eggs, a large marble, a watch, about half-a-dozen of the inevitable glass balls, and then crumpled, crinkled paper, more and more and more, talking all the time of the way in which people neglect to brush their hats INSIDE as well as out, politely, of course, but with a certain personal application. "All sorts of things accumulate, sir.... Not YOU, of course, in particular.... Nearly every customer.... Astonishing what they carry about with them...." The crumpled paper rose and billowed on the counter more and more and more, until he was nearly hidden from us, until he was altogether hidden, and still his voice went on and on. "We none of us know what the fair semblance of a human being may conceal, sir. Are we all then no better than brushed exteriors, whited sepulchres—"

His voice stopped—exactly like when you hit a neighbour's gramophone with a well-aimed brick, the same instant silence, and the rustle of the paper stopped, and everything was still....

"Have you done with my hat?" I said, after an interval.

There was no answer.

I stared at Gip, and Gip stared at me, and there were our distortions in the magic mirrors, looking very rum, and grave, and quiet....

"I think we'll go now," I said. "Will you tell me how much all this comes to?...."

"I say," I said, on a rather louder note, "I want the bill; and my hat, please."

It might have been a sniff from behind the paper pile....

"Let's look behind the counter, Gip," I said. "He's making fun of us."

I led Gip round the head-wagging tiger, and what do you think there was behind the counter? No one at all! Only my hat on the floor, and a common conjurer's lop-eared white rabbit lost in meditation, and looking as stupid and crumpled as only a conjurer's rabbit can do. I resumed my hat, and the rabbit lolloped a lollop or so out of my way.

"Dadda!" said Gip, in a guilty whisper.

"What is it, Gip?" said I.

"I DO like this shop, dadda."

"So should I," I said to myself, "if the counter wouldn't suddenly extend itself to shut one off from the door." But I didn't call Gip's attention to that. "Pussy!" he said, with a hand out to the rabbit as it came lolloping past us; "Pussy, do Gip a magic!" and his eyes followed it as it squeezed through a door I had certainly not remarked a moment before. Then this door opened wider, and the man with one ear larger than the other appeared again. He was smiling still, but his eye met mine with something between amusement and defiance. "You'd like to see our show-room, sir," he said, with an innocent suavity. Gip tugged my finger forward. I glanced at the counter and met the shopman's eye again. I was beginning to think the magic just a little too genuine. "We haven't VERY much time," I said. But somehow we were inside the show-room before I could finish that.

"All goods of the same quality," said the shopman, rubbing his flexible hands together, "and that is the Best. Nothing in the place that isn't genuine Magic, and warranted thoroughly rum. Excuse me, sir!"

I felt him pull at something that clung to my coat-sleeve, and then I saw he held a little, wriggling red demon by the tail—the little creature bit and fought and tried to get at his hand—and in a moment he tossed it carelessly behind a counter. No doubt the thing was only an image of twisted indiarubber, but for the moment—! And his gesture was exactly that of a man who handles some petty biting bit of vermin. I glanced at Gip, but Gip was looking at a magic rocking-horse. I was glad he hadn't seen the thing. "I say," I said, in an undertone, and indicating Gip and the red demon with my eyes, "you haven't many things like THAT about, have you?"

"None of ours! Probably brought it with you," said the shopman—also in an undertone, and with a more dazzling smile than ever. "Astonishing what people WILL carry about with them unawares!" And then to Gip, "Do you see anything you fancy here?"

There were many things that Gip fancied there.

He turned to this astonishing tradesman with mingled confidence and respect. "Is that a Magic Sword?" he said.

"A Magic Toy Sword. It neither bends, breaks, nor cuts the fingers. It renders the bearer invincible in battle against any one under eighteen. Half-a-crown to seven and sixpence, according to size. These panoplies on cards are for juvenile knights-errant and very useful—shield of safety, sandals of swiftness, helmet of invisibility."

"Oh, daddy!" gasped Gip.

I tried to find out what they cost, but the shopman did not heed me. He had got Gip now; he had got him away from my finger; he had embarked upon the exposition of all his confounded stock, and nothing was going to stop him. Presently I saw with a qualm of distrust and something very like jealousy that Gip had hold of this person's finger as usually he has hold of mine. No doubt the fellow was interesting, I thought, and had an interestingly faked lot of stuff, really GOOD faked stuff, still—

I wandered after them, saying very little, but keeping an eye on this prestidigital fellow. After all, Gip was enjoying it. And no doubt when the time came to go we should be able to go quite easily.

It was a long, rambling place, that show-room, a gallery broken up by stands and stalls and pillars, with archways leading off to other departments, in which the queerest-looking assistants loafed and stared at one, and with perplexing mirrors and curtains. So perplexing, indeed, were these that I was presently unable to make out the door by which we had come.

The shopman showed Gip magic trains that ran without steam or clockwork, just as you set the signals, and then some very, very valuable boxes of soldiers that all came alive directly you took off the lid and said—. I myself haven't a very quick ear and it was a tongue-twisting sound, but Gip—he has his mother's ear—got it in no time. "Bravo!" said the shopman, putting the men back into the box unceremoniously and handing it to Gip. "Now," said the shopman, and in a moment Gip had made them all alive again.

"You'll take that box?" asked the shopman.

"We'll take that box," said I, "unless you charge its full value. In which case it would need a Trust Magnate—"

"Dear heart! NO!" and the shopman swept the little men back again, shut the lid, waved the box in the air, and there it was, in brown paper, tied up and—WITH GIP'S FULL NAME AND ADDRESS ON THE PAPER!

The shopman laughed at my amazement.

"This is the genuine magic," he said. "The real thing."

"It's a little too genuine for my taste," I said again.

After that he fell to showing Gip tricks, odd tricks, and still odder the way they were done. He explained them, he turned them inside out, and there was the dear little chap nodding his busy bit of a head in the sagest manner.

I did not attend as well as I might. "Hey, presto!" said the Magic Shopman, and then would come the clear, small "Hey, presto!" of the boy. But I was distracted by other things. It was being borne in upon me just how tremendously rum this place was; it was, so to speak, inundated by a sense of rumness. There was something a little rum about the fixtures even, about the ceiling, about the floor, about the casually distributed chairs. I had a queer feeling that whenever I wasn't looking at them straight they went askew, and moved about, and played a noiseless puss-in-the-corner behind my back. And the cornice had a serpentine design with masks—masks altogether too expressive for proper plaster.

Then abruptly my attention was caught by one of the odd-looking assistants. He was some way off and evidently unaware of my presence—I saw a sort of three-quarter length of him over a pile of toys and through an arch—and, you know, he was leaning against a pillar in an idle sort of way doing the most horrid things with his features! The particular horrid thing he did was with his nose. He did it just as though he was idle and wanted to amuse himself. First of all it was a short, blobby nose, and then suddenly he shot it out like a telescope, and then out it flew and became thinner and thinner until it was like a long, red, flexible whip. Like a thing in a nightmare it was! He flourished it about and flung it forth as a fly-fisher flings his line.

My instant thought was that Gip mustn't see him. I turned about, and there was Gip quite preoccupied with the shopman, and thinking no evil. They were whispering together and looking at me. Gip was standing on a little stool, and the shopman was holding a sort of big drum in his hand.

"Hide and seek, dadda!" cried Gip. "You're He!"

And before I could do anything to prevent it, the shopman had clapped the big drum over him. I saw what was up directly. "Take that off," I cried, "this instant! You'll frighten the boy. Take it off!"

The shopman with the unequal ears did so without a word, and held the big cylinder towards me to show its emptiness. And the little stool was vacant! In that instant my boy had utterly disappeared?...

You know, perhaps, that sinister something that comes like a hand out of the unseen and grips your heart about. You know it takes your common self away and leaves you tense and deliberate, neither slow nor hasty, neither angry nor afraid. So it was with me.

I came up to this grinning shopman and kicked his stool aside.

"Stop this folly!" I said. "Where is my boy?"

"You see," he said, still displaying the drum's interior, "there is no deception——"

I put out my hand to grip him, and he eluded me by a dexterous movement. I snatched again, and he turned from me and pushed open a door to escape. "Stop!" I said, and he laughed, receding. I leapt after him—into utter darkness.

THUD!

"Lor' bless my 'eart! I didn't see you coming, sir!"

I was in Regent Street, and I had collided with a decent-looking working man; and a yard away, perhaps, and looking a little perplexed with himself, was Gip. There was some sort of apology, and then Gip had turned and come to me with a bright little smile, as though for a moment he had missed me.

And he was carrying four parcels in his arm!

He secured immediate possession of my finger.

For the second I was rather at a loss. I stared round to see the door of the magic shop, and, behold, it was not there! There was no door, no shop, nothing, only the common pilaster between the shop where they sell pictures and the window with the chicks!...

I did the only thing possible in that mental tumult; I walked straight to the kerbstone and held up my umbrella for a cab.

"'Ansoms," said Gip, in a note of culminating exultation.

I helped him in, recalled my address with an effort, and got in also. Something unusual proclaimed itself in my tail-coat pocket, and I felt and discovered a glass ball. With a petulant expression I flung it into the street.

Gip said nothing.

For a space neither of us spoke.

"Dada!" said Gip, at last, "that WAS a proper shop!"

I came round with that to the problem of just how the whole thing had seemed to him. He looked completely undamaged—so far, good; he was neither scared nor unhinged, he was simply tremendously satisfied with the afternoon's entertainment, and there in his arms were the four parcels.

Confound it! what could be in them?

"Um!" I said. "Little boys can't go to shops like that every day."

He received this with his usual stoicism, and for a moment I was sorry I was his father and not his mother, and so couldn't suddenly there, coram publico, in our hansom, kiss him. After all, I thought, the thing wasn't so very bad.

But it was only when we opened the parcels that I really began to be reassured. Three of them contained boxes of soldiers, quite ordinary lead soldiers, but of so good a quality as to make Gip altogether forget that originally these parcels had been Magic Tricks of the only genuine sort, and the fourth contained a kitten, a little living white kitten, in excellent health and appetite and temper.

I saw this unpacking with a sort of provisional relief. I hung about in the nursery for quite an unconscionable time....

That happened six months ago. And now I am beginning to believe it is all right. The kitten had only the magic natural to all kittens, and the soldiers seem as steady a company as any colonel could desire. And Gip—?

The intelligent parent will understand that I have to go cautiously with Gip.

But I went so far as this one day. I said, "How would you like your soldiers to come alive, Gip, and march about by themselves?"

"Mine do," said Gip. "I just have to say a word I know before I open the lid."

"Then they march about alone?"

"Oh, QUITE, dadda. I shouldn't like them if they didn't do that."

I displayed no unbecoming surprise, and since then I have taken occasion to drop in upon him once or twice, unannounced, when the soldiers were about, but so far I have never discovered them performing in anything like a magical manner.

It's so difficult to tell.

There's also a question of finance. I have an incurable habit of paying bills. I have been up and down Regent Street several times, looking for that shop. I am inclined to think, indeed, that in that matter honour is satisfied, and that, since Gip's name and address are known to them, I may very well leave it to these people, whoever they may be, to send in their bill in their own time.

3. THE VALLEY OF SPIDERS

Towards mid-day the three pursuers came abruptly round a bend in the torrent bed upon the sight of a very broad and spacious valley. The difficult and winding trench of pebbles along which they had tracked the fugitives for so long, expanded to a broad slope, and with a common impulse the three men left the trail, and rode to a little eminence set with olive-dun trees, and there halted, the two others, as became them, a little behind the man with the silver-studded bridle.

For a space they scanned the great expanse below them with eager eyes. It spread remoter and remoter, with only a few clusters of sere thorn bushes here and there, and the dim suggestions of some now waterless ravine, to break its desolation of yellow grass. Its purple distances melted at last into the bluish slopes of the further hills—hills it might be of a greener kind— and above them invisibly supported, and seeming indeed to hang in the blue, were the snowclad summits of mountains that grew larger and bolder to the north-westward as the sides of the valley drew together. And westward the valley opened until a distant darkness under the sky told where the forests began. But the three men looked neither east nor west, but only steadfastly across the valley.

The gaunt man with the scarred lip was the first to speak. "Nowhere," he said, with a sigh of disappointment in his voice. "But after all, they had a full day's start."

"They don't know we are after them," said the little man on the white horse.

"SHE would know," said the leader bitterly, as if speaking to himself.

"Even then they can't go fast. They've got no beast but the mule, and all to-day the girl's foot has been bleeding——"

The man with the silver bridle flashed a quick intensity of rage on him. "Do you think I haven't seen that?" he snarled.

"It helps, anyhow," whispered the little man to himself.

The gaunt man with the scarred lip stared impassively. "They can't be over the valley," he said. "If we ride hard—"

He glanced at the white horse and paused.

"Curse all white horses!" said the man with the silver bridle, and turned to scan the beast his curse included.

The little man looked down between the melancholy ears of his steed.

"I did my best," he said.

The two others stared again across the valley for a space. The gaunt man passed the back of his hand across the scarred lip.

"Come up!" said the man who owned the silver bridle, suddenly. The little man started and jerked his rein, and the horse hoofs of the three made a multitudinous faint pattering upon the withered grass as they turned back towards the trail....

They rode cautiously down the long slope before them, and so came through a waste of prickly, twisted bushes and strange dry shapes of horny branches that grew amongst the rocks, into the levels below. And there the trail grew faint, for the soil was scanty, and the only herbage was this scorched dead straw that lay upon the ground. Still, by hard scanning, by leaning beside the horses' necks and pausing ever and again, even these white men could contrive to follow after their prey.

There were trodden places, bent and broken blades of the coarse grass, and ever and again the sufficient intimation of a footmark. And once the leader saw a brown smear of blood where the half-caste girl may have trod. And at that under his breath he cursed her for a fool.

The gaunt man checked his leader's tracking, and the little man on the white horse rode behind, a man lost in a dream. They rode one after another, the man with the silver bridle led the way, and they spoke never a word. After a time it came to the little man on the white horse that the world was very still. He started out of his dream. Besides the little noises of their horses and equipment, the whole great valley kept the brooding quiet of a painted scene.

Before him went his master and his fellow, each intently leaning forward to the left, each impassively moving with the paces of his horse; their shadows went before them—still, noiseless, tapering attendants; and nearer a crouched cool shape was his own. He looked about him. What was it had gone? Then he remembered the reverberation from the banks of the gorge and the perpetual accompaniment of shifting, jostling pebbles. And, moreover—? There was no breeze. That was it! What a vast, still place it was, a monotonous afternoon slumber. And the sky open and blank, except for a sombre veil of haze that had gathered in the upper valley.

He straightened his back, fretted with his bridle, puckered his lips to whistle, and simply sighed. He turned in his saddle for a time, and stared at the throat of the mountain gorge out of which they had come. Blank! Blank slopes on either side, with never a sign of a decent beast or tree—much less a man. What a land it was! What a wilderness! He dropped again into his former pose.

It filled him with a momentary pleasure to see a wry stick of purple black flash out into the form of a snake, and vanish amidst the brown. After all, the infernal valley WAS alive. And then, to rejoice him still more, came a little breath across his face, a whisper that came and went, the faintest inclination of a stiff black-antlered bush upon a little crest, the first intimations of a possible breeze. Idly he wetted his finger, and held it up.

He pulled up sharply to avoid a collision with the gaunt man, who had stopped at fault upon the trail. Just at that guilty moment he caught his master's eye looking towards him.

For a time he forced an interest in the tracking. Then, as they rode on again, he studied his master's shadow and hat and shoulder, appearing and disappearing behind the gaunt man's nearer contours. They had ridden four days out of the very limits of the world into this desolate place, short of water, with nothing but a strip of dried meat under their saddles, over rocks and mountains, where surely none but these fugitives had ever been before—for THAT!

And all this was for a girl, a mere wilful child! And the man had whole cityfuls of people to do his basest bidding—girls, women! Why in the name of passionate folly THIS one in particular? asked the little man, and scowled at the world, and licked his parched lips with a blackened tongue. It was the way of the master, and that was all he knew. Just because she sought to evade him....

His eye caught a whole row of high plumed canes bending in unison, and then the tails of silk that hung before his neck flapped and fell. The breeze was growing stronger. Somehow it took the stiff stillness out of things—and that was well.

"Hullo!" said the gaunt man.

All three stopped abruptly.

"What?" asked the master. "What?"

"Over there," said the gaunt man, pointing up the valley.

"What?"

"Something coming towards us."

And as he spoke a yellow animal crested a rise and came bearing down upon them. It was a big wild dog, coming before the wind, tongue out, at a steady pace, and running with such an intensity of purpose that he did not seem to see the horsemen he approached. He ran with his nose up, following, it was plain, neither scent nor quarry. As he drew nearer the little man felt for his sword. "He's mad," said the gaunt rider.

"Shout!" said the little man, and shouted.

The dog came on. Then when the little man's blade was already out, it swerved aside and went panting by them and past. The eyes of the little man followed its flight. "There was no foam," he said. For a space the man with the silver-studded bridle stared up the valley. "Oh, come on!" he cried at last. "What does it matter?" and jerked his horse into movement again.

The little man left the insoluble mystery of a dog that fled from nothing but the wind, and lapsed into profound musings on human character. "Come on!" he whispered to himself. "Why should it be given to one man to say 'Come on!' with that stupendous violence of effect. Always, all his life, the man with the silver bridle has been saying that. If *I* said it—!" thought the little man. But people marvelled when the master was disobeyed even in the wildest things. This half-caste girl seemed to him, seemed to every one, mad—blasphemous almost. The little man, by way of comparison, reflected on the gaunt rider with the scarred lip, as stalwart as his master, as brave and, indeed, perhaps braver, and yet for him there was obedience, nothing but to give obedience duly and stoutly...

Certain sensations of the hands and knees called the little man back to more immediate things. He became aware of something. He rode up beside his gaunt fellow. "Do you notice the horses?" he said in an undertone.

The gaunt face looked interrogation.

"They don't like this wind," said the little man, and dropped behind as the man with the silver bridle turned upon him.

"It's all right," said the gaunt-faced man.

They rode on again for a space in silence. The foremost two rode downcast upon the trail, the hindmost man watched the haze that crept down the vastness of the valley, nearer and nearer, and noted how the wind grew in strength moment by moment. Far away on the left he saw a line of dark bulks—wild hog perhaps, galloping down the valley, but of that he said nothing, nor did he remark again upon the uneasiness of the horses.

And then he saw first one and then a second great white ball, a great shining white ball like a gigantic head of thistle-down, that drove before the wind athwart the path. These balls soared high in the air, and dropped and rose again and caught for a moment, and hurried on and passed, but at the sight of them the restlessness of the horses increased.

Then presently he saw that more of these drifting globes—and then soon very many more—were hurrying towards him down the valley.

They became aware of a squealing. Athwart the path a huge boar rushed, turning his head but for one instant to glance at them, and then hurling on down the valley again. And at that, all three stopped and sat in their saddles, staring into the thickening haze that was coming upon them.

"If it were not for this thistle-down—" began the leader.

But now a big globe came drifting past within a score of yards of them. It was really not an even sphere at all, but a vast, soft, ragged, filmy thing, a sheet gathered by the corners, an aerial jelly-fish, as it were, but rolling over and over as it advanced, and trailing long, cobwebby threads and streamers that floated in its wake.

"It isn't thistle-down," said the little man.

"I don't like the stuff," said the gaunt man.

And they looked at one another.

"Curse it!" cried the leader. "The air's full of it up there. If it keeps on at this pace long, it will stop us altogether."

An instinctive feeling, such as lines out a herd of deer at the approach of some ambiguous thing, prompted them to turn their horses to the wind, ride forward for a few paces, and stare at that advancing multitude of floating masses. They came on before the wind with a sort of smooth swiftness, rising and falling noiselessly, sinking to earth, rebounding high, soaring—all with a perfect unanimity, with a still, deliberate assurance.

Right and left of the horsemen the pioneers of this strange army passed. At one that rolled along the ground, breaking shapelessly and trailing out reluctantly into long grappling ribbons and bands, all three horses began to shy and dance. The master was seized with a sudden unreasonable impatience. He cursed the drifting globes roundly. "Get on!" he cried; "get on! What do these things matter? How CAN they matter? Back to the trail!" He fell swearing at his horse and sawed the bit across its mouth.

He shouted aloud with rage. "I will follow that trail, I tell you!" he cried. "Where is the trail?"

He gripped the bridle of his prancing horse and searched amidst the grass. A long and clinging thread fell across his face, a grey streamer dropped about his bridle-arm, some big, active thing with many legs ran down the back of his head. He looked up to discover one of those grey masses anchored as it were above him by these things and flapping out ends as a sail flaps when a boat comes, about—but noiselessly.

He had an impression of many eyes, of a dense crew of squat bodies, of long, many-jointed limbs hauling at their mooring ropes to bring the thing down upon him. For a space he stared up, reining in his prancing horse with the instinct born of years of horsemanship. Then the flat of a sword smote his back, and a blade flashed overhead and cut the drifting balloon of spider-web free, and the whole mass lifted softly and drove clear and away.

"Spiders!" cried the voice of the gaunt man. "The things are full of big spiders! Look, my lord!"

The man with the silver bridle still followed the mass that drove away.

"Look, my lord!"

The master found himself staring down at a red, smashed thing on the ground that, in spite of partial obliteration, could still wriggle unavailing legs. Then when the gaunt man pointed to another mass that bore down upon them, he drew his sword hastily. Up the valley now it was like a fog bank torn to rags. He tried to grasp the situation.

"Ride for it!" the little man was shouting. "Ride for it down the valley."

What happened then was like the confusion of a battle. The man with the silver bridle saw the little man go past him slashing furiously at imaginary cobwebs, saw him cannon into the horse of the gaunt man and hurl it and its rider to earth. His own horse went a dozen paces before he could rein it in. Then he looked up to avoid imaginary dangers, and then back again to see a horse rolling on the ground, the gaunt man standing and slashing over it at a rent and fluttering mass of grey that streamed and wrapped about them both. And thick and fast as thistle-down on waste land on a windy day in July, the cobweb masses were coming on.

The little man had dismounted, but he dared not release his horse. He was endeavouring to lug the struggling brute back with the strength of one arm, while with the other he slashed aimlessly, The tentacles of a second grey mass had entangled themselves with the struggle, and this second grey mass came to its moorings, and slowly sank.

The master set his teeth, gripped his bridle, lowered his head, and spurred his horse forward. The horse on the ground rolled over, there were blood and moving shapes upon the flanks, and the gaunt man, suddenly leaving it, ran forward towards his master, perhaps ten paces. His legs were swathed and encumbered with grey; he made ineffectual movements with his sword. Grey streamers waved from him; there was a thin veil of grey across his face. With his left hand he beat at something on his body, and suddenly he stumbled and fell. He struggled to rise, and fell again, and suddenly, horribly, began to howl, "Oh—ohoo, ohooh!"

The master could see the great spiders upon him, and others upon the ground.

As he strove to force his horse nearer to this gesticulating, screaming grey object that struggled up and down, there came a clatter of hoofs, and the little man, in act of mounting, swordless, balanced on his belly athwart the white horse, and clutching its mane, whirled past. And again a clinging thread of grey gossamer swept across the master's face. All about him, and over him, it seemed this drifting, noiseless cobweb circled and drew nearer him....

To the day of his death he never knew just how the event of that moment happened. Did he, indeed, turn his horse, or did it really of its own accord stampede after its fellow? Suffice it that in another second he was galloping full tilt down the valley with his sword whirling furiously overhead. And all about him on the quickening breeze, the spiders' airships, their air bundles and air sheets, seemed to him to hurry in a conscious pursuit.

Clatter, clatter, thud, thud—the man with the silver bridle rode, heedless of his direction, with his fearful face looking up now right, now left, and his sword arm ready to slash. And a few hundred yards ahead of him, with a tail of torn cobweb trailing behind him, rode the little man on the white horse, still but imperfectly in the saddle. The reeds bent before them, the wind blew fresh and strong, over his shoulder the master could see the webs hurrying to overtake....

He was so intent to escape the spiders' webs that only as his horse gathered together for a leap did he realise the ravine ahead. And then he realised it only to misunderstand and interfere. He was leaning forward on his horse's neck and sat up and back all too late.

But if in his excitement he had failed to leap, at any rate he had not forgotten how to fall. He was horseman again in mid-air. He came off clear with a mere bruise upon his shoulder, and his horse rolled, kicking spasmodic legs, and lay still. But the master's sword drove its point into the hard soil, and snapped clean across, as though Chance refused him any longer as her Knight, and the splintered end missed his face by an inch or so.

He was on his feet in a moment, breathlessly scanning the onrushing spider-webs. For a moment he was minded to run, and then thought of the ravine, and turned back. He ran aside once to dodge one drifting terror, and then he was swiftly clambering down the precipitous sides, and out of the touch of the gale.

There under the lee of the dry torrent's steeper banks he might crouch, and watch these strange, grey masses pass and pass in safety till the wind fell, and it became possible to escape. And there for a long time he crouched, watching the strange, grey, ragged masses trail their streamers across his narrowed sky.

Once a stray spider fell into the ravine close beside him—a full foot it measured from leg to leg, and its body was half a man's hand—and after he had watched its monstrous alacrity of search and escape for a little while, and tempted it to bite his broken sword, he lifted up his iron-heeled boot and smashed it into a pulp. He swore as he did so, and for a time sought up and down for another.

Then presently, when he was surer these spider swarms could not drop into the ravine, he found a place where he could sit down, and sat and fell into deep thought and began after his manner to gnaw his knuckles and bite his nails. And from this he was moved by the coming of the man with the white horse.

He heard him long before he saw him, as a clattering of hoofs, stumbling footsteps, and a reassuring voice. Then the little man appeared, a rueful figure, still with a tail of white cobweb trailing behind him. They approached each other without speaking, without a salutation. The little man was fatigued and shamed to the pitch of hopeless bitterness, and came to a stop at last, face to face with his seated master. The latter winced a little under his dependant's eye. "Well?" he said at last, with no pretence of authority.

"You left him?"

"My horse bolted."

"I know. So did mine."

He laughed at his master mirthlessly.

"I say my horse bolted," said the man who once had a silver-studded bridle.

"Cowards both," said the little man.

The other gnawed his knuckle through some meditative moments, with his eye on his inferior.

"Don't call me a coward," he said at length.

"You are a coward like myself."

"A coward possibly. There is a limit beyond which every man must fear. That I have learnt at last. But not like yourself. That is where the difference comes in."

"I never could have dreamt you would have left him. He saved your life two minutes before.... Why are you our lord?"

The master gnawed his knuckles again, and his countenance was dark.

"No man calls me a coward," he said. "No. A broken sword is better than none.... One spavined white horse cannot be expected to carry two men a four days' journey. I hate white horses, but this time it cannot be helped. You begin to understand me?... I perceive that you are minded, on the strength of what you have seen and fancy, to taint my reputation. It is men of your sort who unmake kings. Besides which—I never liked you."

"My lord!" said the little man.

"No," said the master. "NO!"

He stood up sharply as the little man moved. For a minute perhaps they faced one another. Overhead the spiders' balls went driving. There was a quick movement among the pebbles; a running of feet, a cry of despair, a gasp and a blow....

Towards nightfall the wind fell. The sun set in a calm serenity, and the man who had once possessed the silver bridle came at last very cautiously and by an easy slope out of the ravine again; but now he led the white horse that once belonged to the little man. He would have gone back to his horse to get his silver-mounted bridle again, but he feared night and a quickening breeze might still find him in the valley, and besides he disliked greatly to think he might discover his horse all swathed in cobwebs and perhaps unpleasantly eaten.

And as he thought of those cobwebs and of all the dangers he had been through, and the manner in which he had been preserved that day, his hand sought a little reliquary that hung about his neck, and he clasped it for a moment with heartfelt gratitude. As he did so his eyes went across the valley.

"I was hot with passion," he said, "and now she has met her reward. They also, no doubt—"

And behold! Far away out of the wooded slopes across the valley, but in the clearness of the sunset distinct and unmistakable, he saw a little spire of smoke.

At that his expression of serene resignation changed to an amazed anger. Smoke? He turned the head of the white horse about, and hesitated. And as he did so a little rustle of air went through the grass about him. Far away upon some reeds swayed a tattered sheet of grey. He looked at the cobwebs; he looked at the smoke.

"Perhaps, after all, it is not them," he said at last.

But he knew better.

After he had stared at the smoke for some time, he mounted the white horse.

As he rode, he picked his way amidst stranded masses of web. For some reason there were many dead spiders on the ground, and those that lived feasted guiltily on their fellows. At the sound of his horse's hoofs they fled.

Their time had passed. From the ground without either a wind to carry them or a winding sheet ready, these things, for all their poison, could do him little evil. He flicked with his belt at those he fancied came too near. Once, where a number ran together over a bare place, he was minded to dismount and trample them with his boots, but this impulse he overcame. Ever and again he turned in his saddle, and looked back at the smoke.

"Spiders," he muttered over and over again. "Spiders! Well, well.... The next time I must spin a web."

4. THE TRUTH ABOUT PYECRAFT

He sits not a dozen yards away. If I glance over my shoulder I can see him. And if I catch his eye—and usually I catch his eye—it meets me with an expression.

It is mainly an imploring look—and yet with suspicion in it.

Confound his suspicion! If I wanted to tell on him I should have told long ago. I don't tell and I don't tell, and he ought to feel at his ease. As if anything so gross and fat as he could feel at ease! Who would believe me if I did tell?

Poor old Pyecraft! Great, uneasy jelly of substance! The fattest clubman in London.

He sits at one of the little club tables in the huge bay by the fire, stuffing. What is he stuffing? I glance judiciously and catch him biting at a round of hot buttered tea-cake, with his eyes on me. Confound him!—with his eyes on me!

That settles it, Pyecraft! Since you WILL be abject, since you WILL behave as though I was not a man of honour, here, right under your embedded eyes, I write the thing down—the plain truth about Pyecraft. The man I helped, the man I shielded, and who has requited me by making my club unendurable, absolutely unendurable, with his liquid appeal, with the perpetual "don't tell" of his looks.

And, besides, why does he keep on eternally eating?

Well, here goes for the truth, the whole truth, and nothing but the truth!

Pyecraft—. I made the acquaintance of Pyecraft in this very smoking-room. I was a young, nervous new member, and he saw it. I was sitting all alone, wishing I knew more of the members, and suddenly he came, a great rolling front of chins and abdomina, towards me, and grunted and sat down in a chair close by me and wheezed for a space, and scraped for a space with a match and lit a cigar, and then addressed me. I forget what he said—something about the matches not lighting properly, and afterwards as he talked he kept stopping the waiters one by one as they went by, and telling them about the matches in that thin, fluty voice he has. But, anyhow, it was in some such way we began our talking.

He talked about various things and came round to games. And thence to my figure and complexion. "YOU ought to be a good cricketer," he said. I suppose I am slender, slender to what some people would call lean, and I suppose I am rather dark, still—I am not ashamed of having a Hindu great-grandmother, but, for all that, I don't want casual strangers to see through me at a glance to HER. So that I was set against Pyecraft from the beginning.

But he only talked about me in order to get to himself.

"I expect," he said, "you take no more exercise than I do, and probably you eat no less." (Like all excessively obese people he fancied he ate nothing.) "Yet,"—and he smiled an oblique smile—"we differ."

And then he began to talk about his fatness and his fatness; all he did for his fatness and all he was going to do for his fatness; what people had advised him to do for his fatness and what he had heard of people doing for fatness similar to his. "A priori," he said, "one would think a question of nutrition could be answered by dietary and a question of assimilation by drugs." It was stifling. It was dumpling talk. It made me feel swelled to hear him.

One stands that sort of thing once in a way at a club, but a time came when I fancied I was standing too much. He took to me altogether too conspicuously. I could never go into the smoking-room but he would come wallowing towards me, and sometimes he came and gormandised round and about me while I had my lunch. He seemed at times almost to be clinging to me. He was a bore, but not so fearful a bore as to be limited to me; and from the first there was something in his manner—almost as though he knew, almost as though he penetrated to the fact that I MIGHT—that there was a remote, exceptional chance in me that no one else presented.

"I'd give anything to get it down," he would say—"anything," and peer at me over his vast cheeks and pant.

Poor old Pyecraft! He has just gonged, no doubt to order another buttered tea-cake!

He came to the actual thing one day. "Our Pharmacopoeia," he said, "our Western Pharmacopoeia, is anything but the last word of medical science. In the East, I've been told—"

He stopped and stared at me. It was like being at an aquarium.

I was quite suddenly angry with him. "Look here," I said, "who told you about my great-grandmother's recipes?"

"Well," he fenced.

"Every time we've met for a week," I said, "and we've met pretty often—you've given me a broad hint or so about that little secret of mine."

"Well," he said, "now the cat's out of the bag, I'll admit, yes, it is so. I had it—"

"From Pattison?"

"Indirectly," he said, which I believe was lying, "yes."

"Pattison," I said, "took that stuff at his own risk."

He pursed his mouth and bowed.

"My great-grandmother's recipes," I said, "are queer things to handle. My father was near making me promise—"

"He didn't?"

"No. But he warned me. He himself used one—once."

"Ah!... But do you think—? Suppose—suppose there did happen to be one—"

"The things are curious documents," I said.

"Even the smell of 'em.... No!"

But after going so far Pyecraft was resolved I should go farther. I was always a little afraid if I tried his patience too much he would fall on me suddenly and smother me. I own I was weak. But I was also annoyed with Pyecraft. I had got to that state of feeling for him that disposed me to say, "Well, TAKE the risk!" The little affair of Pattison to which I have alluded was a different matter altogether. What it was doesn't concern us now, but I knew, anyhow, that the particular recipe I used then was safe. The rest I didn't know so much about, and, on the whole, I was inclined to doubt their safety pretty completely.

Yet even if Pyecraft got poisoned—

I must confess the poisoning of Pyecraft struck me as an immense undertaking.

That evening I took that queer, odd-scented sandalwood box out of my safe and turned the rustling skins over. The gentleman who wrote the recipes for my great-grandmother evidently had a weakness for skins of a miscellaneous origin, and his handwriting was cramped to the last degree. Some of the things are quite unreadable to me—though my family, with its Indian Civil Service associations, has kept up a knowledge of Hindustani from generation to generation—and none are absolutely plain sailing. But I found the one that I knew was there soon enough, and sat on the floor by my safe for some time looking at it.

"Look here," said I to Pyecraft next day, and snatched the slip away from his eager grasp.

"So far as I—can make it out, this is a recipe for Loss of Weight. ("Ah!" said Pyecraft.) I'm not absolutely sure, but I think it's that. And if you take my advice you'll leave it alone. Because, you know—I blacken my blood in your interest, Pyecraft—my ancestors on that side were, so far as I can gather, a jolly queer lot. See?"

"Let me try it," said Pyecraft.

I leant back in my chair. My imagination made one mighty effort and fell flat within me. "What in Heaven's name, Pyecraft," I asked, "do you think you'll look like when you get thin?"

He was impervious to reason. I made him promise never to say a word to me about his disgusting fatness again whatever happened—never, and then I handed him that little piece of skin.

"It's nasty stuff," I said.

"No matter," he said, and took it.

He goggled at it. "But—but—" he said.

He had just discovered that it wasn't English.

"To the best of my ability," I said, "I will do you a translation."

I did my best. After that we didn't speak for a fortnight. Whenever he approached me I frowned and motioned him away, and he respected our compact, but at the end of a fortnight he was as fat as ever. And then he got a word in.

"I must speak," he said. "It isn't fair. There's something wrong. It's done me no good. You're not doing your great-grandmother justice."

"Where's the recipe?"

He produced it gingerly from his pocket-book.

I ran my eye over the items. "Was the egg addled?" I asked.

"No. Ought it to have been?"

"That," I said, "goes without saying in all my poor dear great-grandmother's recipes. When condition or quality is not specified you must get the worst. She was drastic or nothing.... And there's one or two possible alternatives to some of these other things. You got FRESH rattlesnake venom."

"I got a rattlesnake from Jamrach's. It cost—it cost—"

"That's your affair, anyhow. This last item—"

"I know a man who—"

"Yes. H'm. Well, I'll write the alternatives down. So far as I know the language, the spelling of this recipe is particularly atrocious. By-the-bye, dog here probably means pariah dog."

For a month after that I saw Pyecraft constantly at the club and as fat and anxious as ever. He kept our treaty, but at times he broke the spirit of it by shaking his head despondently. Then one day in the cloakroom he said, "Your great-grandmother—"

"Not a word against her," I said; and he held his peace.

I could have fancied he had desisted, and I saw him one day talking to three new members about his fatness as though he was in search of other recipes. And then, quite unexpectedly, his telegram came.

"Mr. Formalyn!" bawled a page-boy under my nose, and I took the telegram and opened it at once.

"For Heaven's sake come.—Pyecraft."

"H'm," said I, and to tell the truth I was so pleased at the rehabilitation of my great grandmother's reputation this evidently promised that I made a most excellent lunch.

I got Pyecraft's address from the hall porter. Pyecraft inhabited the upper half of a house in Bloomsbury, and I went there so soon as I had done my coffee and Trappistine. I did not wait to finish my cigar.

"Mr. Pyecraft?" said I, at the front door.

They believed he was ill; he hadn't been out for two days.

"He expects me," said I, and they sent me up.

I rang the bell at the lattice-door upon the landing.

"He shouldn't have tried it, anyhow," I said to myself. "A man who eats like a pig ought to look like a pig."

An obviously worthy woman, with an anxious face and a carelessly placed cap, came and surveyed me through the lattice.

I gave my name and she let me in in a dubious fashion.

"Well?" said I, as we stood together inside Pyecraft's piece of the landing.

"'E said you was to come in if you came," she said, and regarded me, making no motion to show me anywhere. And then, confidentially, "'E's locked in, sir."

"Locked in?"

"Locked himself in yesterday morning and 'asn't let any one in since, sir. And ever and again SWEARING. Oh, my!"

I stared at the door she indicated by her glances.

"In there?" I said.

"Yes, sir."

"What's up?"

She shook her head sadly, "'E keeps on calling for vittles, sir. 'EAVY vittles 'e wants. I get 'im what I can. Pork 'e's 'ad, sooit puddin', sossiges, noo bread. Everythink like that. Left outside, if you please, and me go away. 'E's eatin', sir, somethink AWFUL."

There came a piping bawl from inside the door: "That Formalyn?"

"That you, Pyecraft?" I shouted, and went and banged the door.

"Tell her to go away."

I did.

Then I could hear a curious pattering upon the door, almost like some one feeling for the handle in the dark, and Pyecraft's familiar grunts.

"It's all right," I said, "she's gone."

But for a long time the door didn't open.

I heard the key turn. Then Pyecraft's voice said, "Come in."

I turned the handle and opened the door. Naturally I expected to see Pyecraft.

Well, you know, he wasn't there!

I never had such a shock in my life. There was his sitting-room in a state of untidy disorder, plates and dishes among the books and writing things, and several chairs overturned, but Pyecraft—

"It's all right, o' man; shut the door," he said, and then I discovered him.

There he was right up close to the cornice in the corner by the door, as though some one had glued him to the ceiling. His face was anxious and angry. He panted and gesticulated. "Shut the door," he said. "If that woman gets hold of it—"

I shut the door, and went and stood away from him and stared.

"If anything gives way and you tumble down," I said, "you'll break your neck, Pyecraft."

"I wish I could," he wheezed.

"A man of your age and weight getting up to kiddish gymnastics—"

"Don't," he said, and looked agonised.

"I'll tell you," he said, and gesticulated.

"How the deuce," said I, "are you holding on up there?"

And then abruptly I realised that he was not holding on at all, that he was floating up there—just as a gas-filled bladder might have floated in the same position. He began a struggle to thrust himself away from the ceiling and to clamber down the wall to me. "It's that prescription," he panted, as he did so. "Your great-gran—"

He took hold of a framed engraving rather carelessly as he spoke and it gave way, and he flew back to the ceiling again, while the picture smashed onto the sofa. Bump he went against the ceiling, and I knew then why he was all over white on the more salient curves and angles of his person. He tried again more carefully, coming down by way of the mantel.

It was really a most extraordinary spectacle, that great, fat, apoplectic-looking man upside down and trying to get from the ceiling to the floor. "That prescription," he said. "Too successful."

"How?"

"Loss of weight—almost complete."

And then, of course, I understood.

"By Jove, Pyecraft," said I, "what you wanted was a cure for fatness! But you always called it weight. You would call it weight."

Somehow I was extremely delighted. I quite liked Pyecraft for the time. "Let me help you!" I said, and took his hand and pulled him down. He kicked about, trying to get a foothold somewhere. It was very like holding a flag on a windy day.

"That table," he said, pointing, "is solid mahogany and very heavy. If you can put me under that—-"

I did, and there he wallowed about like a captive balloon, while I stood on his hearthrug and talked to him.

I lit a cigar. "Tell me," I said, "what happened?"

"I took it," he said.

"How did it taste?"

"Oh, BEASTLY!"

I should fancy they all did. Whether one regards the ingredients or the probable compound or the possible results, almost all of my great-grandmother's remedies appear to me at least to be extraordinarily uninviting. For my own part—

"I took a little sip first."

"Yes?"

"And as I felt lighter and better after an hour, I decided to take the draught."

"My dear Pyecraft!"

"I held my nose," he explained. "And then I kept on getting lighter and lighter—and helpless, you know."

He gave way to a sudden burst of passion. "What the goodness am I to DO?" he said.

"There's one thing pretty evident," I said, "that you mustn't do. If you go out of doors, you'll go up and up." I waved an arm upward. "They'd have to send Santos-Dumont after you to bring you down again."

"I suppose it will wear off?"

I shook my head. "I don't think you can count on that," I said.

And then there was another burst of passion, and he kicked out at adjacent chairs and banged the floor. He behaved just as I should have expected a great, fat, self-indulgent man to behave under trying circumstances—that is to say, very badly. He spoke of me and my great-grandmother with an utter want of discretion.

"I never asked you to take the stuff," I said.

And generously disregarding the insults he was putting upon me, I sat down in his armchair and began to talk to him in a sober, friendly fashion.

I pointed out to him that this was a trouble he had brought upon himself, and that it had almost an air of poetical justice. He had eaten too much. This he disputed, and for a time we argued the point.

He became noisy and violent, so I desisted from this aspect of his lesson. "And then," said I, "you committed the sin of euphuism. You called it not Fat, which is just and inglorious, but Weight. You—"

He interrupted to say he recognised all that. What was he to DO?

I suggested he should adapt himself to his new conditions. So we came to the really sensible part of the business. I suggested that it would not be difficult for him to learn to walk about on the ceiling with his hands—

"I can't sleep," he said.

But that was no great difficulty. It was quite possible, I pointed out, to make a shake-up under a wire mattress, fasten the under things on with tapes, and have a blanket, sheet, and coverlet to button at the side. He would have to confide in his housekeeper, I said; and after some squabbling he agreed to that. (Afterwards it was quite delightful to see the beautifully matter-of-fact way with which the good lady took all these amazing inversions.) He could have a library ladder in his room, and all his meals could be laid on the top of his bookcase. We also hit on an ingenious device by which he could get to the floor whenever he wanted, which was simply to put the British Encyclopaedia (tenth edition) on the top of his open shelves. He just pulled out a couple of volumes and held on, and down he came. And we agreed there must be iron staples along the skirting, so that he could cling to those whenever he wanted to get about the room on the lower level.

As we got on with the thing I found myself almost keenly interested. It was I who called in the housekeeper and broke matters to her, and it was I chiefly who fixed up the inverted bed. In fact, I spent two whole days at his flat. I am a handy, interfering sort of man with a screw-driver, and I made all sorts of ingenious adaptations for him—ran a wire to bring his bells within reach, turned all his electric lights up instead of down, and so on. The whole affair was extremely curious and interesting to me, and it was delightful to think of Pyecraft like some great, fat blow-fly, crawling about on his ceiling and clambering round the lintels of his doors from one room to another, and never, never, never coming to the club any more....

Then, you know, my fatal ingenuity got the better of me. I was sitting by his fire drinking his whisky, and he was up in his favourite corner by the cornice, tacking a Turkey carpet to the ceiling, when the idea struck me. "By Jove, Pyecraft!" I said, "all this is totally unnecessary."

And before I could calculate the complete consequences of my notion I blurted it out. "Lead underclothing," said I, and the mischief was done.

Pyecraft received the thing almost in tears. "To be right ways up again—" he said. I gave him the whole secret before I saw where it would take me. "Buy sheet lead," I said, "stamp it into discs. Sew 'em all over your underclothes until you have enough. Have lead-soled boots, carry a bag of solid lead, and the thing is done! Instead of being a prisoner here you may go abroad again, Pyecraft; you may travel—"

A still happier idea came to me. "You need never fear a shipwreck. All you need do is just slip off some or all of your clothes, take the necessary amount of luggage in your hand, and float up in the air—"

In his emotion he dropped the tack-hammer within an ace of my head. "By Jove!" he said, "I shall be able to come back to the club again."

The thing pulled me up short. "By Jove!" I said faintly. "Yes. Of course—you will."

He did. He does. There he sits behind me now, stuffing—as I live!—a third go of buttered tea-cake. And no one in the whole world knows—except his housekeeper and me—that he weighs practically nothing; that he is a mere boring mass of assimilatory matter, mere clouds in clothing, niente, nefas, the most inconsiderable of men. There he sits watching until I have done this writing. Then, if he can, he will waylay me. He will come billowing up to me....

He will tell me over again all about it, how it feels, how it doesn't feel, how he sometimes hopes it is passing off a little. And always somewhere in that fat, abundant discourse he will say, "The secret's keeping, eh? If any one knew of it—I should be so ashamed.... Makes a fellow look such a fool, you know. Crawling about on a ceiling and all that...."

And now to elude Pyecraft, occupying, as he does, an admirable strategic position between me and the door.

5. MR. SKELMERSDALE IN FAIRYLAND

"There's a man in that shop," said the Doctor, "who has been in Fairyland."

"Nonsense!" I said, and stared back at the shop. It was the usual village shop, post-office, telegraph wire on its brow, zinc pans and brushes outside, boots, shirtings, and potted meats in the window. "Tell me about it," I said, after a pause.

"*I* don't know," said the Doctor. "He's an ordinary sort of lout—Skelmersdale is his name. But everybody about here believes it like Bible truth."

I reverted presently to the topic.

"I know nothing about it," said the Doctor, "and I don't WANT to know. I attended him for a broken finger—Married and Single cricket match—and that's when I struck the nonsense. That's all. But it shows you the sort of stuff I have to deal with, anyhow, eh? Nice to get modern sanitary ideas into a people like this!"

"Very," I said in a mildly sympathetic tone, and he went on to tell me about that business of the Bonham drain. Things of that kind, I observe, are apt to weigh on the minds of Medical Officers of Health. I was as sympathetic as I knew how, and when he called the Bonham people "asses," I said they were "thundering asses," but even that did not allay him.

Afterwards, later in the summer, an urgent desire to seclude myself, while finishing my chapter on Spiritual Pathology—it was really, I believe, stiffer to write than it is to read—took me to Bignor. I lodged at a farmhouse, and presently found myself outside that little general shop again, in search of tobacco. "Skelmersdale," said I to myself at the sight of it, and went in.

I was served by a short, but shapely, young man, with a fair downy complexion, good, small teeth, blue eyes, and a languid manner. I scrutinised him curiously. Except for a touch of melancholy in his expression, he was nothing out of the common. He was in the shirt-sleeves and tucked-up apron of his trade, and a pencil was thrust behind his inoffensive ear. Athwart his black waistcoat was a gold chain, from which dangled a bent guinea.

"Nothing more to-day, sir?" he inquired. He leant forward over my bill as he spoke.

"Are you Mr. Skelmersdale?" said I.

"I am, sir," he said, without looking up.

"Is it true that you have been in Fairyland?"

He looked up at me for a moment with wrinkled brows, with an aggrieved, exasperated face. "O SHUT it!" he said, and, after a moment of hostility, eye to eye, he went on adding up my bill. "Four, six and a half," he said, after a pause. "Thank you, Sir."

So, unpropitiously, my acquaintance with Mr. Skelmersdale began.

Well, I got from that to confidence—through a series of toilsome efforts. I picked him up again in the Village Room, where of a night I went to play billiards after my supper, and mitigate the extreme seclusion from my kind that was so helpful to work during the day. I contrived to play with him and afterwards to talk with him. I found the one subject to avoid was Fairyland. On everything else he was open and amiable in a commonplace sort of way, but on that he had been worried—it was a manifest taboo. Only once in the room did I hear the slightest allusion to his experience in his presence, and that was by a cross-grained farm hand who was losing to him. Skelmersdale had run a break into double figures, which, by the Bignor standards, was uncommonly good play. "Steady on!" said his adversary. "None of your fairy flukes!"

Skelmersdale stared at him for a moment, cue in hand, then flung it down and walked out of the room.

"Why can't you leave 'im alone?" said a respectable elder who had been enjoying the game, and in the general murmur of disapproval the grin of satisfied wit faded from the ploughboy's face.

I scented my opportunity. "What's this joke," said I, "about Fairyland?"

"'Tain't no joke about Fairyland, not to young Skelmersdale," said the respectable elder, drinking. A little man with rosy cheeks was more communicative. "They DO say, sir," he said, "that they took him into Aldington Knoll an' kep' him there a matter of three weeks."

And with that the gathering was well under weigh. Once one sheep had started, others were ready enough to follow, and in a little time I had at least the exterior aspect of the Skelmersdale affair. Formerly, before he came to Bignor, he had been in that very similar little shop at Aldington Corner, and there whatever it was did happen had taken place. The story was clear that he had stayed out late one night on the Knoll and vanished for three weeks from the sight of men, and had returned with "his cuffs as clean as when he started," and his pockets full of dust and ashes. He returned in a state of moody wretchedness that only slowly passed away, and for many days he would give no account of where it was he had been. The girl he was engaged to at Clapton Hill tried to get it out of him, and threw him over partly because he refused, and partly because, as she said, he fairly gave her the "'ump." And then when, some time after, he let out to some one carelessly that he had been in Fairyland and wanted to go back, and when the thing spread and the simple badinage of the countryside came into play, he threw up his situation abruptly, and came to Bignor to get out of the fuss. But as to what had happened in Fairyland none of these people knew. There the gathering in the Village Room went to pieces like a pack at fault. One said this, and another said that.

Their air in dealing with this marvel was ostensibly critical and sceptical, but I could see a considerable amount of belief showing through their guarded qualifications. I took a line of intelligent interest, tinged with a reasonable doubt of the whole story.

"If Fairyland's inside Aldington Knoll," I said, "why don't you dig it out?"

"That's what I says," said the young ploughboy.

"There's a-many have tried to dig on Aldington Knoll," said the respectable elder, solemnly, "one time and another. But there's none as goes about to-day to tell what they got by digging."

The unanimity of vague belief that surrounded me was rather impressive; I felt there must surely be SOMETHING at the root of so much conviction, and the already pretty keen curiosity I felt about the real facts of the case was distinctly whetted. If these real facts were to be got from any one, they were to be got from Skelmersdale himself; and I set myself, therefore, still more assiduously to efface the first bad impression I had made and win his confidence to the pitch of voluntary speech. In that endeavour I had a social advantage. Being a person of affability and no apparent employment, and wearing tweeds and knickerbockers, I was naturally classed as an artist in Bignor, and in the remarkable code of social precedence prevalent in Bignor an artist ranks considerably higher than a grocer's assistant. Skelmersdale, like too many of his class, is something of a snob; he had told me to "shut it," only under sudden, excessive provocation, and with, I am certain, a subsequent repentance; he was, I knew, quite glad to be seen walking about the village with me. In due course, he accepted the proposal of a pipe and whisky in my rooms readily enough, and there, scenting by some happy instinct that there was trouble of the heart in this, and knowing that confidences beget confidences, I plied him with much of interest and suggestion from my real and fictitious past. And it was after the third whisky of the third visit of that sort, if I remember rightly, that a propos of some artless expansion of a little affair that had touched and left me in my teens, that he did at last, of his own free will and motion, break the ice. "It was like that with me," he said, "over there at Aldington. It's just that that's so rum. First I didn't care a bit and it was all her, and afterwards, when it was too late, it was, in a manner of speaking, all me."

I forbore to jump upon this allusion, and so he presently threw out another, and in a little while he was making it as plain as daylight that the one thing he wanted to talk about now was this Fairyland adventure he had sat tight upon for so long. You see, I'd done the trick with him, and from being just another half-incredulous, would-be facetious stranger, I had, by all my wealth of shameless self-exposure, become the possible confidant. He had been bitten by the desire to show that he, too, had lived and felt many things, and the fever was upon him.

He was certainly confoundedly allusive at first, and my eagerness to clear him up with a few precise questions was only equalled and controlled by my anxiety not to get to this sort of thing too soon. But in another meeting or so the basis of confidence was complete; and from first to last I think I got most of the items and aspects—indeed, I got quite a number of times over almost everything that Mr. Skelmersdale, with his very limited powers of narration, will ever be able to tell. And so I come to the story of his adventure, and I piece it all together again. Whether it really happened, whether he imagined it or dreamt it, or fell upon it in some strange hallucinatory trance, I do not profess to say. But that he invented it I will not for one moment entertain. The man simply and honestly believes the thing happened as he says it happened; he is transparently incapable of any lie so elaborate and sustained, and in the belief of the simple, yet often keenly penetrating, rustic minds about him I find a very strong confirmation of his sincerity. He believes—and nobody can produce any positive fact to falsify his belief. As for me, with this much of endorsement, I transmit his story—I am a little old now to justify or explain.

He says he went to sleep on Aldington Knoll about ten o'clock one night—it was quite possibly Midsummer night, though he has never thought of the date, and he cannot be sure within a week or so—and it was a fine night and windless, with a rising moon. I have been at the pains to visit this Knoll thrice since his story grew up under my persuasions, and once I went there in the twilight summer moonrise on what was, perhaps, a similar night to that of his adventure. Jupiter was great and splendid above the moon, and in the north and northwest the sky was green and vividly bright over the sunken sun. The Knoll stands out bare and bleak under the sky, but surrounded at a little distance by dark thickets, and as I went up towards it there was a mighty starting and scampering of ghostly or quite invisible rabbits. Just over the crown of the Knoll, but nowhere else, was a multitudinous thin trumpeting of midges. The Knoll is, I believe, an artificial mound, the tumulus of some great prehistoric chieftain, and surely no man ever chose a more spacious prospect for a sepulchre. Eastward one sees along the hills to Hythe, and thence across the Channel to where, thirty miles and more perhaps, away, the great white lights by Gris Nez and Boulogne wink and pass and shine.

Westward lies the whole tumbled valley of the Weald, visible as far as Hindhead and Leith Hill, and the valley of the Stour opens the Downs in the north to interminable hills beyond Wye. All Romney Marsh lies southward at one's feet, Dymchurch and Romney and Lydd, Hastings and its hill are in the middle distance, and the hills multiply vaguely far beyond where Eastbourne rolls up to Beachy Head.

And out upon all this it was that Skelmersdale wandered, being troubled in his earlier love affair, and as he says, "not caring WHERE he went." And there he sat down to think it over, and so, sulking and grieving, was overtaken by sleep. And so he fell into the fairies' power.

The quarrel that had upset him was some trivial matter enough between himself and the girl at Clapton Hill to whom he was engaged. She was a farmer's daughter, said Skelmersdale, and "very respectable," and no doubt an excellent match for him; but both girl and lover were very young and with just that mutual jealousy, that intolerantly keen edge of criticism, that irrational hunger for a beautiful perfection, that life and wisdom do presently and most mercifully dull. What the precise matter of quarrel was I have no idea. She may have said she liked men in gaiters when he hadn't any gaiters on, or he may have said he liked her better in a different sort of hat, but however it began, it got by a series of clumsy stages to bitterness and tears. She no doubt got tearful and smeary, and he grew dusty and drooping, and she parted with invidious comparisons, grave doubts whether she ever had REALLY cared for him, and a clear certainty she would never care again. And with this sort of thing upon his mind he came out upon Aldington Knoll grieving, and presently, after a long interval, perhaps, quite inexplicably, fell asleep.

He woke to find himself on a softer turf than ever he had slept on before, and under the shade of very dark trees that completely hid the sky. Always, indeed, in Fairyland the sky is hidden, it seems. Except for one night when the fairies were dancing, Mr. Skelmersdale, during all his time with them, never saw a star. And of that night I am in doubt whether he was in Fairyland proper or out where the rings and rushes are, in those low meadows near the railway line at Smeeth.

But it was light under these trees for all that, and on the leaves and amidst the turf shone a multitude of glow-worms, very bright and fine. Mr. Skelmersdale's first impression was that he was SMALL, and the next that quite a number of people still smaller were standing all about him. For some reason, he says, he was neither surprised nor frightened, but sat up quite deliberately and rubbed the sleep out of his eyes. And there all about him stood the smiling elves who had caught him sleeping under their privileges and had brought him into Fairyland.

What these elves were like I have failed to gather, so vague and imperfect is his vocabulary, and so unobservant of all minor detail does he seem to have been. They were clothed in something very light and beautiful, that was neither wool, nor silk, nor leaves, nor the petals of flowers. They stood all about him as he sat and waked, and down the glade towards him, down a glow-worm avenue and fronted by a star, came at once that Fairy Lady who is the chief personage of his memory and tale. Of her I gathered more. She was clothed in filmy green, and about her little waist was a broad silver girdle. Her hair waved back from her forehead on either side; there were curls not too wayward and yet astray, and on her brow was a little tiara, set with a single star. Her sleeves were some sort of open sleeves that gave little glimpses of her arms; her throat, I think, was a little displayed, because he speaks of the beauty of her neck and chin. There was a necklace of coral about her white throat, and in her breast a coral-coloured flower. She had the soft lines of a little child in her chin and cheeks and throat. And her eyes, I gather, were of a kindled brown, very soft and straight and sweet under her level brows. You see by these particulars how greatly this lady must have loomed in Mr. Skelmersdale's picture. Certain things he tried to express and could not express; "the way she moved," he said several times; and I fancy a sort of demure joyousness radiated from this Lady.

And it was in the company of this delightful person, as the guest and chosen companion of this delightful person, that Mr. Skelmersdale set out to be taken into the intimacies of Fairyland. She welcomed him gladly and a little warmly—I suspect a pressure of his hand in both of hers and a lit face to his. After all, ten years ago young Skelmersdale may have been a very comely youth. And once she took his arm, and once, I think, she led him by the hand adown the glade that the glow-worms lit.

Just how things chanced and happened there is no telling from Mr. Skelmersdale's disarticulated skeleton of description. He gives little unsatisfactory glimpses of strange corners and doings, of places where there were many fairies together, of "toadstool things that shone pink," of fairy food, of which he could only say "you should have tasted it!" and of fairy music, "like a little musical box," that came out of nodding flowers. There was a great open place where fairies rode and raced on "things," but what Mr. Skelmersdale meant by "these here things they rode," there is no telling. Larvae, perhaps, or crickets, or the little beetles that elude us so abundantly. There was a place where water splashed and gigantic king-cups grew, and there in the hotter times the fairies bathed together. There were games being played and dancing and much elvish love-making, too, I think, among the moss-branch thickets. There can be no doubt that the Fairy Lady made love to Mr. Skelmersdale, and no doubt either that this young man set himself to resist her. A time came, indeed, when she sat on a bank beside him, in a quiet, secluded place "all smelling of vi'lets," and talked to him of love.

"When her voice went low and she whispered," said Mr. Skelmersdale, "and laid 'er 'and on my 'and, you know, and came close with a soft, warm friendly way she 'ad, it was as much as I could do to keep my 'ead."

It seems he kept his head to a certain limited unfortunate extent. He saw "'ow the wind was blowing," he says, and so, sitting there in a place all smelling of violets, with the touch of this lovely Fairy Lady about him, Mr. Skelmersdale broke it to her gently—that he was engaged!

She had told him she loved him dearly, that he was a sweet human lad for her, and whatever he would ask of her he should have—even his heart's desire.

And Mr. Skelmersdale, who, I fancy, tried hard to avoid looking at her little lips as they just dropped apart and came together, led up to the more intimate question by saying he would like enough capital to start a little shop. He'd just like to feel, he said, he had money enough to do that. I imagine a little surprise in those brown eyes he talked about, but she seemed sympathetic for all that, and she asked him many questions about the little shop, "laughing like" all the time. So he got to the complete statement of his affianced position, and told her all about Millie.

"All?" said I.

"Everything," said Mr. Skelmersdale, "just who she was, and where she lived, and everything about her. I sort of felt I 'ad to all the time, I did."

"'Whatever you want you shall have,' said the Fairy Lady. 'That's as good as done. You SHALL feel you have the money just as you wish. And now, you know—YOU MUST KISS ME.'"

And Mr. Skelmersdale pretended not to hear the latter part of her remark, and said she was very kind. That he really didn't deserve she should be so kind. And—

The Fairy Lady suddenly came quite close to him and whispered, "Kiss me!"

"And," said Mr. Skelmersdale, "like a fool, I did."

There are kisses and kisses, I am told, and this must have been quite the other sort from Millie's resonant signals of regard. There was something magic in that kiss; assuredly it marked a turning point. At any rate, this is one of the passages that he thought sufficiently important to describe most at length. I have tried to get it right, I have tried to disentangle it from the hints and gestures through which it came to me, but I have no doubt that it was all different from my telling and far finer and sweeter, in the soft filtered light and the subtly stirring silences of the fairy glades. The Fairy Lady asked him more about Millie, and was she very lovely, and so on—a great many times. As to Millie's loveliness, I conceive him answering that she was "all right." And then, or on some such occasion, the Fairy Lady told him she had fallen in love with him as he slept in the moonlight, and so he had been brought into Fairyland, and she had thought, not knowing of Millie, that perhaps he might chance to love her. "But now you know you can't," she said, "so you must stop with me just a little while, and then you must go back to Millie." She told him that, and you know Skelmersdale was already in love with her, but the pure inertia of his mind kept him in the way he was going. I imagine him sitting in a sort of stupefaction amidst all these glowing beautiful things, answering about his Millie and the little shop he projected and the need of a horse and cart.... And that absurd state of affairs must have gone on for days and days. I see this little lady, hovering about him and trying to amuse him, too dainty to understand his complexity and too tender to let him go. And he, you know, hypnotised as it were by his earthly position, went his way with her hither and thither, blind to everything in Fairyland but this wonderful intimacy that had come to him. It is hard, it is impossible, to give in print the effect of her radiant sweetness shining through the jungle of poor Skelmersdale's rough and broken sentences. To me, at least, she shone clear amidst the muddle of his story like a glow-worm in a tangle of weeds.

There must have been many days of things while all this was happening—and once, I say, they danced under the moonlight in the fairy rings that stud the meadows near Smeeth—but at last it all came to an end. She led him into a great cavernous place, lit by a red nightlight sort of thing, where there were coffers piled on coffers, and cups and golden boxes, and a great heap of what certainly seemed to all Mr. Skelmersdale's senses—coined gold. There were little gnomes amidst this wealth, who saluted her at her coming, and stood aside. And suddenly she turned on him there with brightly shining eyes.

"And now," she said, "you have been kind to stay with me so long, and it is time I let you go. You must go back to your Millie. You must go back to your Millie, and here—just as I promised you—they will give you gold."

"She choked like," said Mr. Skelmersdale. "At that, I had a sort of feeling—" (he touched his breastbone) "as though I was fainting here. I felt pale, you know, and shivering, and even then—I 'adn't a thing to say."

He paused. "Yes," I said.

The scene was beyond his describing. But I know that she kissed him good-bye.

"And you said nothing?"

"Nothing," he said. "I stood like a stuffed calf. She just looked back once, you know, and stood smiling like and crying—I could see the shine of her eyes—and then she was gone, and there was all these little fellows bustling about me, stuffing my 'ands and my pockets and the back of my collar and everywhere with gold."

And then it was, when the Fairy Lady had vanished, that Mr. Skelmersdale really understood and knew. He suddenly began plucking out the gold they were thrusting upon him, and shouting out at them to prevent their giving him more. "'I don't WANT yer gold,' I said. 'I 'aven't done yet. I'm not going. I want to speak to that Fairy Lady again.' I started off to go after her and they held me back. Yes, stuck their little 'ands against my middle and shoved me back. They kept giving me more and more gold until it was running all down my trouser legs and dropping out of my 'ands. 'I don't WANT yer gold,' I says to them, 'I want just to speak to the Fairy Lady again.'"

"And did you?"

"It came to a tussle."

"Before you saw her?"

"I didn't see her. When I got out from them she wasn't anywhere to be seen."

So he ran in search of her out of this red-lit cave, down a long grotto, seeking her, and thence he came out in a great and desolate place athwart which a swarm of will-o'-the-wisps were flying to and fro. And about him elves were dancing in derision, and the little gnomes came out of the cave after him, carrying gold in handfuls and casting it after him, shouting, "Fairy love and fairy gold! Fairy love and fairy gold!"

And when he heard these words, came a great fear that it was all over, and he lifted up his voice and called to her by her name, and suddenly set himself to run down the slope from the mouth of the cavern, through a place of thorns and briers, calling after her very loudly and often. The elves danced about him unheeded, pinching him and pricking him, and the will-o'-the-wisps circled round him and dashed into his face, and the gnomes pursued him shouting and pelting him with fairy gold. As he ran with all this strange rout about him and distracting him, suddenly he was knee-deep in a swamp, and suddenly he was amidst thick twisted roots, and he caught his foot in one and stumbled and fell....

He fell and he rolled over, and in that instant he found himself sprawling upon Aldington Knoll, all lonely under the stars.

He sat up sharply at once, he says, and found he was very stiff and cold, and his clothes were damp with dew. The first pallor of dawn and a chilly wind were coming up together. He could have believed the whole thing a strangely vivid dream until he thrust his hand into his side pocket and found it stuffed with ashes. Then he knew for certain it was fairy gold they had given him. He could feel all their pinches and pricks still, though there was never a bruise upon him. And in that manner, and so suddenly, Mr. Skelmersdale came out of Fairyland back into this world of men. Even then he fancied the thing was but the matter of a night until he returned to the shop at Aldington Corner and discovered amidst their astonishment that he had been away three weeks.

"Lor'! the trouble I 'ad!" said Mr. Skelmersdale.

"How?"

"Explaining. I suppose you've never had anything like that to explain."

"Never," I said, and he expatiated for a time on the behaviour of this person and that. One name he avoided for a space.

"And Millie?" said I at last.

"I didn't seem to care a bit for seeing Millie," he said.

"I expect she seemed changed?"

"Every one was changed. Changed for good. Every one seemed big, you know, and coarse. And their voices seemed loud. Why, the sun, when it rose in the morning, fair hit me in the eye!"

"And Millie?"

"I didn't want to see Millie."

"And when you did?"

"I came up against her Sunday, coming out of church. 'Where you been?' she said, and I saw there was a row. *I* didn't care if there was. I seemed to forget about her even while she was there a-talking to me. She was just nothing. I couldn't make out whatever I 'ad seen in 'er ever, or what there could 'ave been. Sometimes when she wasn't about, I did get back a little, but never when she was there. Then it was always the other came up and blotted her out.... Anyow, it didn't break her heart."

"Married?" I asked.

"Married 'er cousin," said Mr. Skelmersdale, and reflected on the pattern of the tablecloth for a space.

When he spoke again it was clear that his former sweetheart had clean vanished from his mind, and that the talk had brought back the Fairy Lady triumphant in his heart. He talked of her—soon he was letting out the oddest things, queer love secrets it would be treachery to repeat. I think, indeed, that was the queerest thing in the whole affair, to hear that neat little grocer man after his story was done, with a glass of whisky beside him and a cigar between his fingers, witnessing, with sorrow still, though now, indeed, with a time-blunted anguish, of the inappeasable hunger of the heart that presently came upon him. "I couldn't eat," he said, "I couldn't sleep. I made mistakes in orders and got mixed with change. There she was day and night, drawing me and drawing me. Oh, I wanted her. Lord! how I wanted her! I was up there, most evenings I was up there on the Knoll, often even when it rained. I used to walk over the Knoll and round it and round it, calling for them to let me in. Shouting. Near blubbering I was at times. Daft I was and miserable. I kept on saying it was all a mistake. And every Sunday afternoon I went up there, wet and fine, though I knew as well as you do it wasn't no good by day. And I've tried to go to sleep there."

He stopped sharply and decided to drink some whisky.

"I've tried to go to sleep there," he said, and I could swear his lips trembled. "I've tried to go to sleep there, often and often. And, you know, I couldn't, sir—never. I've thought if I could go to sleep there, there might be something. But I've sat up there and laid up there, and I couldn't—not for thinking and longing. It's the longing.... I've tried—"

He blew, drank up the rest of his whisky spasmodically, stood up suddenly and buttoned his jacket, staring closely and critically at the cheap oleographs beside the mantel meanwhile. The little black notebook in which he recorded the orders of his daily round projected stiffly from his breast pocket. When all the buttons were quite done, he patted his chest and turned on me suddenly. "Well," he said, "I must be going."

There was something in his eyes and manner that was too difficult for him to express in words. "One gets talking," he said at last at the door, and smiled wanly, and so vanished from my eyes. And that is the tale of Mr. Skelmersdale in Fairyland just as he told it to me.

6. THE STORY OF THE INEXPERIENCED GHOST

The scene amidst which Clayton told his last story comes back very vividly to my mind. There he sat, for the greater part of the time, in the corner of the authentic settle by the spacious open fire, and Sanderson sat beside him smoking the Broseley clay that bore his name. There was Evans, and that marvel among actors, Wish, who is also a modest man. We had all come down to the Mermaid Club that Saturday morning, except Clayton, who had slept there overnight—which indeed gave him the opening of his story. We had golfed until golfing was invisible; we had dined, and we were in that mood of tranquil kindliness when men will suffer a story. When Clayton began to tell one, we naturally supposed he was lying. It may be that indeed he was lying—of that the reader will speedily be able to judge as well as I. He began, it is true, with an air of matter-of-fact anecdote, but that we thought was only the incurable artifice of the man.

"I say!" he remarked, after a long consideration of the upward rain of sparks from the log that Sanderson had thumped, "you know I was alone here last night?"

"Except for the domestics," said Wish.

"Who sleep in the other wing," said Clayton. "Yes. Well—" He pulled at his cigar for some little time as though he still hesitated about his confidence. Then he said, quite quietly, "I caught a ghost!"

"Caught a ghost, did you?" said Sanderson. "Where is it?"

And Evans, who admires Clayton immensely and has been four weeks in America, shouted, "CAUGHT a ghost, did you, Clayton? I'm glad of it! Tell us all about it right now."

Clayton said he would in a minute, and asked him to shut the door.

He looked apologetically at me. "There's no eavesdropping of course, but we don't want to upset our very excellent service with any rumours of ghosts in the place. There's too much shadow and oak panelling to trifle with that. And this, you know, wasn't a regular ghost. I don't think it will come again—ever."

"You mean to say you didn't keep it?" said Sanderson.

"I hadn't the heart to," said Clayton.

And Sanderson said he was surprised.

We laughed, and Clayton looked aggrieved. "I know," he said, with the flicker of a smile, "but the fact is it really WAS a ghost, and I'm as sure of it as I am that I am talking to you now. I'm not joking. I mean what I say."

Sanderson drew deeply at his pipe, with one reddish eye on Clayton, and then emitted a thin jet of smoke more eloquent than many words.

Clayton ignored the comment. "It is the strangest thing that has ever happened in my life. You know, I never believed in ghosts or anything of the sort, before, ever; and then, you know, I bag one in a corner; and the whole business is in my hands."

He meditated still more profoundly, and produced and began to pierce a second cigar with a curious little stabber he affected.

"You talked to it?" asked Wish.

"For the space, probably, of an hour."

"Chatty?" I said, joining the party of the sceptics.

"The poor devil was in trouble," said Clayton, bowed over his cigar-end and with the very faintest note of reproof.

"Sobbing?" some one asked.

Clayton heaved a realistic sigh at the memory. "Good Lord!" he said; "yes." And then, "Poor fellow! yes."

"Where did you strike it?" asked Evans, in his best American accent.

"I never realised," said Clayton, ignoring him, "the poor sort of thing a ghost might be," and he hung us up again for a time, while he sought for matches in his pocket and lit and warmed to his cigar.

"I took an advantage," he reflected at last.

We were none of us in a hurry. "A character," he said, "remains just the same character for all that it's been disembodied. That's a thing we too often forget. People with a certain strength or fixity of purpose may have ghosts of a certain strength and fixity of purpose—most haunting ghosts, you know, must be as one-idea'd as monomaniacs and as obstinate as mules to come back again and again. This poor creature wasn't." He suddenly looked up rather queerly, and his eye went round the room. "I say it," he said, "in all kindliness, but that is the plain truth of the case. Even at the first glance he struck me as weak."

He punctuated with the help of his cigar.

"I came upon him, you know, in the long passage. His back was towards me and I saw him first. Right off I knew him for a ghost. He was transparent and whitish; clean through his chest I could see the glimmer of the little window at the end. And not only his physique but his attitude struck me as being weak. He looked, you know, as though he didn't know in the slightest whatever he meant to do. One hand was on the panelling and the other fluttered to his mouth. Like—SO!"

"What sort of physique?" said Sanderson.

"Lean. You know that sort of young man's neck that has two great flutings down the back, here and here—so! And a little, meanish head with scrubby hair—And rather bad ears. Shoulders bad, narrower than the hips; turn-down collar, ready-made short jacket, trousers baggy and a little frayed at the heels. That's how he took me. I came very quietly up the staircase. I did not carry a light, you know—the candles are on the landing table and there is that lamp—and I was in my list slippers, and I saw him as I came up. I stopped dead at that—taking him in. I wasn't a bit afraid. I think that in most of these affairs one is never nearly so afraid or excited as one imagines one would be. I was surprised and interested. I thought, 'Good Lord! Here's a ghost at last! And I haven't believed for a moment in ghosts during the last five-and-twenty years.'"

"Um," said Wish.

"I suppose I wasn't on the landing a moment before he found out I was there. He turned on me sharply, and I saw the face of an immature young man, a weak nose, a scrubby little moustache, a feeble chin. So for an instant we stood—he looking over his shoulder at me and regarded one another. Then he seemed to remember his high calling. He turned round, drew himself up, projected his face, raised his arms, spread his hands in approved ghost fashion—came towards me. As he did so his little jaw dropped, and he emitted a faint, drawn-out 'Boo.' No, it wasn't—not a bit dreadful. I'd dined. I'd had a bottle of champagne, and being all alone, perhaps two or three—perhaps even four or five—whiskies, so I was as solid as rocks and no more frightened than if I'd been assailed by a frog. 'Boo!' I said. 'Nonsense. You don't belong to THIS place. What are you doing here?'

"I could see him wince. 'Boo-oo,' he said.

"'Boo—be hanged! Are you a member?' I said; and just to show I didn't care a pin for him I stepped through a corner of him and made to light my candle. 'Are you a member?' I repeated, looking at him sideways.

"He moved a little so as to stand clear of me, and his bearing became crestfallen. 'No,' he said, in answer to the persistent interrogation of my eye; 'I'm not a member—I'm a ghost.'

"'Well, that doesn't give you the run of the Mermaid Club. Is there any one you want to see, or anything of that sort?' and doing it as steadily as possible for fear that he should mistake the carelessness of whisky for the distraction of fear, I got my candle alight. I turned on him, holding it. 'What are you doing here?' I said.

"He had dropped his hands and stopped his booing, and there he stood, abashed and awkward, the ghost of a weak, silly, aimless young man. 'I'm haunting,' he said.

"'You haven't any business to,' I said in a quiet voice.

"'I'm a ghost,' he said, as if in defence.

"'That may be, but you haven't any business to haunt here. This is a respectable private club; people often stop here with nursemaids and children, and, going about in the careless way you do, some poor little mite could easily come upon you and be scared out of her wits. I suppose you didn't think of that?'

"'No, sir,' he said, 'I didn't.'

"'You should have done. You haven't any claim on the place, have you? Weren't murdered here, or anything of that sort?'

"'None, sir; but I thought as it was old and oak-panelled—'

"'That's NO excuse.' I regarded him firmly. 'Your coming here is a mistake,' I said, in a tone of friendly superiority. I feigned to see if I had my matches, and then looked up at him frankly. 'If I were you I wouldn't wait for cock-crow—I'd vanish right away.'

"He looked embarrassed. 'The fact IS, sir—' he began.

"'I'd vanish,' I said, driving it home.

"'The fact is, sir, that—somehow—I can't.'

"'You CAN'T?'

"'No, sir. There's something I've forgotten. I've been hanging about here since midnight last night, hiding in the cupboards of the empty bedrooms and things like that. I'm flurried. I've never come haunting before, and it seems to put me out.'

"'Put you out?'

"'Yes, sir. I've tried to do it several times, and it doesn't come off. There's some little thing has slipped me, and I can't get back.'

"That, you know, rather bowled me over. He looked at me in such an abject way that for the life of me I couldn't keep up quite the high, hectoring vein I had adopted. 'That's queer,' I said, and as I spoke I fancied I heard some one moving about down below. 'Come into my room and tell me more about it,' I said. 'I didn't, of course, understand this,' and I tried to take him by the arm. But, of course, you might as well have tried to take hold of a puff of smoke! I had forgotten my number, I think; anyhow, I remember going into several bedrooms—it was lucky I was the only soul in that wing—until I saw my traps. 'Here we are,' I said, and sat down in the arm-chair; 'sit down and tell me all about it. It seems to me you have got yourself into a jolly awkward position, old chap.'

"Well, he said he wouldn't sit down! he'd prefer to flit up and down the room if it was all the same to me. And so he did, and in a little while we were deep in a long and serious talk. And presently, you know, something of those whiskies and sodas evaporated out of me, and I began to realise just a little what a thundering rum and weird business it was that I was in. There he was, semi-transparent—the proper conventional phantom, and noiseless except for his ghost of a voice—flitting to and fro in that nice, clean, chintz-hung old bedroom. You could see the gleam of the copper candlesticks through him, and the lights on the brass fender, and the corners of the framed engravings on the wall,—and there he was telling me all about this wretched little life of his that had recently ended on earth. He hadn't a particularly honest face, you know, but being transparent, of course, he couldn't avoid telling the truth."

"Eh?" said Wish, suddenly sitting up in his chair.

"What?" said Clayton.

"Being transparent—couldn't avoid telling the truth—I don't see it," said Wish.

"*I* don't see it," said Clayton, with inimitable assurance. "But it IS so, I can assure you nevertheless. I don't believe he got once a nail's breadth off the Bible truth. He told me how he had been killed—he went down into a London basement with a candle to look for a leakage of gas—and described himself as a senior English master in a London private school when that release occurred."

"Poor wretch!" said I.

"That's what I thought, and the more he talked the more I thought it. There he was, purposeless in life and purposeless out of it. He talked of his father and mother and his schoolmaster, and all who had ever been anything to him in the world, meanly. He had been too sensitive, too nervous; none of them had ever valued him properly or understood him, he said. He had never had a real friend in the world, I think; he had never had a success. He had shirked games and failed examinations. 'It's like that with some people,' he said; 'whenever I got into the examination-room or anywhere everything seemed to go.' Engaged to be married of course—to another over-sensitive person, I suppose—when the indiscretion with the gas escape ended his affairs. 'And where are you now?' I asked. 'Not in—?'

"He wasn't clear on that point at all. The impression he gave me was of a sort of vague, intermediate state, a special reserve for souls too non-existent for anything so positive as either sin or virtue. *I* don't know. He was much too egotistical and unobservant to give me any clear idea of the kind of place, kind of country, there is on the Other Side of Things. Wherever he was, he seems to have fallen in with a set of kindred spirits: ghosts of weak Cockney young men, who were on a footing of Christian names, and among these there was certainly a lot of talk about 'going haunting' and things like that. Yes—going haunting! They seemed to think 'haunting' a tremendous adventure, and most of them funked it all the time. And so primed, you know, he had come."

"But really!" said Wish to the fire.

"These are the impressions he gave me, anyhow," said Clayton, modestly. "I may, of course, have been in a rather uncritical state, but that was the sort of background he gave to himself. He kept flitting up and down, with his thin voice going talking, talking about his wretched self, and never a word of clear, firm statement from first to last. He was thinner and sillier and more pointless than if he had been real and alive. Only then, you know, he would not have been in my bedroom here—if he HAD been alive. I should have kicked him out."

"Of course," said Evans, "there ARE poor mortals like that."

"And there's just as much chance of their having ghosts as the rest of us," I admitted.

"What gave a sort of point to him, you know, was the fact that he did seem within limits to have found himself out. The mess he had made of haunting had depressed him terribly. He had been told it would be a 'lark'; he had come expecting it to be a 'lark,' and here it was, nothing but another failure added to his record! He proclaimed himself an utter out-and-out failure. He said, and I can quite believe it, that he had never tried to do anything all his life that he hadn't made a perfect mess of—and through all the wastes of eternity he never would. If he had had sympathy, perhaps—. He paused at that, and stood regarding me. He remarked that, strange as it might seem to me, nobody, not any one, ever, had given him the amount of sympathy I was doing now. I could see what he wanted straight away, and I determined to head him off at once. I may be a brute, you know, but being the Only Real Friend, the recipient of the confidences of one of these egotistical weaklings, ghost or body, is beyond my physical endurance. I got up briskly. 'Don't you brood on these things too much,' I said. 'The thing you've got to do is to get out of this get out of this—sharp. You pull yourself together and TRY.' 'I can't,' he said. 'You try,' I said, and try he did."

"Try!" said Sanderson. "HOW?"

"Passes," said Clayton.

"Passes?"

"Complicated series of gestures and passes with the hands. That's how he had come in and that's how he had to get out again. Lord! what a business I had!"

"But how could ANY series of passes—?" I began.

"My dear man," said Clayton, turning on me and putting a great emphasis on certain words, "you want EVERYTHING clear. *I* don't know HOW. All I know is that you DO—that HE did, anyhow, at least. After a fearful time, you know, he got his passes right and suddenly disappeared."

"Did you," said Sanderson, slowly, "observe the passes?"

"Yes," said Clayton, and seemed to think. "It was tremendously queer," he said. "There we were, I and this thin vague ghost, in that silent room, in this silent, empty inn, in this silent little Friday-night town. Not a sound except our voices and a faint panting he made when he swung. There was the bedroom candle, and one candle on the dressing-table alight, that was all—sometimes one or other would flare up into a tall, lean, astonished flame for a space. And queer things happened. 'I can't,' he said; 'I shall never—!' And suddenly he sat down on a little chair at the foot of the bed and began to sob and sob. Lord! what a harrowing, whimpering thing he seemed!

"'You pull yourself together,' I said, and tried to pat him on the back, and... my confounded hand went through him! By that time, you know, I wasn't nearly so—massive as I had been on the landing. I got the queerness of it full. I remember snatching back my hand out of him, as it were, with a little thrill, and walking over to the dressing-table. 'You pull yourself together,' I said to him, 'and try.' And in order to encourage and help him I began to try as well."

"What!" said Sanderson, "the passes?"

"Yes, the passes."

"But—" I said, moved by an idea that eluded me for a space.

"This is interesting," said Sanderson, with his finger in his pipe-bowl. "You mean to say this ghost of yours gave away—"

"Did his level best to give away the whole confounded barrier? YES."

"He didn't," said Wish; "he couldn't. Or you'd have gone there too."

"That's precisely it," I said, finding my elusive idea put into words for me.

"That IS precisely it," said Clayton, with thoughtful eyes upon the fire.

For just a little while there was silence.

"And at last he did it?" said Sanderson.

"At last he did it. I had to keep him up to it hard, but he did it at last—rather suddenly. He despaired, we had a scene, and then he got up abruptly and asked me to go through the whole performance, slowly, so that he might see. 'I believe,' he said, 'if I could SEE I should spot what was wrong at once.' And he did. '*I* know,' he said. 'What do you know?' said I. '*I* know,' he repeated. Then he said, peevishly, 'I CAN'T do it if you look at me—I really CAN'T; it's been that, partly, all along. I'm such a nervous fellow that you put me out.' Well, we had a bit of an argument. Naturally I wanted to see; but he was as obstinate as a mule, and suddenly I had come over as tired as a dog—he tired me out. 'All right,' I said, '*I* won't look at you,' and turned towards the mirror, on the wardrobe, by the bed.

"He started off very fast. I tried to follow him by looking in the looking-glass, to see just what it was had hung. Round went his arms and his hands, so, and so, and so, and then with a rush came to the last gesture of all—you stand erect and open out your arms—and so, don't you know, he stood. And then he didn't! He didn't! He wasn't! I wheeled round from the looking-glass to him. There was nothing, I was alone, with the flaring candles and a staggering mind. What had happened? Had anything happened? Had I been dreaming?... And then, with an absurd note of finality about it, the clock upon the landing discovered the moment was ripe for striking ONE. So!—Ping! And I was as grave and sober as a judge, with all my champagne and whisky gone into the vast serene. Feeling queer, you know—confoundedly QUEER! Queer! Good Lord!"

He regarded his cigar-ash for a moment. "That's all that happened," he said.

"And then you went to bed?" asked Evans.

"What else was there to do?"

I looked Wish in the eye. We wanted to scoff, and there was something, something perhaps in Clayton's voice and manner, that hampered our desire.

"And about these passes?" said Sanderson.

"I believe I could do them now."

"Oh!" said Sanderson, and produced a penknife and set himself to grub the dottel out of the bowl of his clay.

"Why don't you do them now?" said Sanderson, shutting his pen-knife with a click.

"That's what I'm going to do," said Clayton.

"They won't work," said Evans.

"If they do—" I suggested.

"You know, I'd rather you didn't," said Wish, stretching out his legs.

"Why?" asked Evans.

"I'd rather he didn't," said Wish.

"But he hasn't got 'em right," said Sanderson, plugging too much tobacco in his pipe.

"All the same, I'd rather he didn't," said Wish.

We argued with Wish. He said that for Clayton to go through those gestures was like mocking a serious matter. "But you don't believe—?" I said. Wish glanced at Clayton, who was staring into the fire, weighing something in his mind. "I do—more than half, anyhow, I do," said Wish.

"Clayton," said I, "you're too good a liar for us. Most of it was all right. But that disappearance... happened to be convincing. Tell us, it's a tale of cock and bull."

He stood up without heeding me, took the middle of the hearthrug, and faced me. For a moment he regarded his feet thoughtfully, and then for all the rest of the time his eyes were on the opposite wall, with an intent expression. He raised his two hands slowly to the level of his eyes and so began....

Now, Sanderson is a Freemason, a member of the lodge of the Four Kings, which devotes itself so ably to the study and elucidation of all the mysteries of Masonry past and present, and among the students of this lodge Sanderson is by no means the least. He followed Clayton's motions with a singular interest in his reddish eye. "That's not bad," he said, when it was done. "You really do, you know, put things together, Clayton, in a most amazing fashion. But there's one little detail out."

"I know," said Clayton. "I believe I could tell you which."

"Well?"

"This," said Clayton, and did a queer little twist and writhing and thrust of the hands.

"Yes."

"That, you know, was what HE couldn't get right," said Clayton. "But how do YOU—?"

"Most of this business, and particularly how you invented it, I don't understand at all," said Sanderson, "but just that phase—I do." He reflected. "These happen to be a series of gestures—connected with a certain branch of esoteric Masonry. Probably you know. Or else—HOW?" He reflected still further. "I do not see I can do any harm in telling you just the proper twist. After all, if you know, you know; if you don't, you don't."

"I know nothing," said Clayton, "except what the poor devil let out last night."

"Well, anyhow," said Sanderson, and placed his churchwarden very carefully upon the shelf over the fireplace. Then very rapidly he gesticulated with his hands.

"So?" said Clayton, repeating.

"So," said Sanderson, and took his pipe in hand again.

"Ah, NOW," said Clayton, "I can do the whole thing—right."

He stood up before the waning fire and smiled at us all. But I think there was just a little hesitation in his smile. "If I begin—" he said.

"I wouldn't begin," said Wish.

"It's all right!" said Evans. "Matter is indestructible. You don't think any jiggery-pokery of this sort is going to snatch Clayton into the world of shades. Not it! You may try, Clayton, so far as I'm concerned, until your arms drop off at the wrists."

"I don't believe that," said Wish, and stood up and put his arm on Clayton's shoulder. "You've made me half believe in that story somehow, and I don't want to see the thing done!"

"Goodness!" said I, "here's Wish frightened!"

"I am," said Wish, with real or admirably feigned intensity. "I believe that if he goes through these motions right he'll GO."

"He'll not do anything of the sort," I cried. "There's only one way out of this world for men, and Clayton is thirty years from that. Besides... And such a ghost! Do you think—?"

Wish interrupted me by moving. He walked out from among our chairs and stopped beside the tole and stood there. "Clayton," he said, "you're a fool."

Clayton, with a humorous light in his eyes, smiled back at him. "Wish," he said, "is right and all you others are wrong. I shall go. I shall get to the end of these passes, and as the last swish whistles through the air, Presto!—this hearthrug will be vacant, the room will be blank amazement, and a respectably dressed gentleman of fifteen stone will plump into the world of shades. I'm certain. So will you be. I decline to argue further. Let the thing be tried."

"NO," said Wish, and made a step and ceased, and Clayton raised his hands once more to repeat the spirit's passing.

By that time, you know, we were all in a state of tension—largely because of the behaviour of Wish. We sat all of us with our eyes on Clayton—I, at least, with a sort of tight, stiff feeling about me as though from the back of my skull to the middle of my thighs my body had been changed to steel. And there, with a gravity that was imperturbably serene, Clayton bowed and swayed and waved his hands and arms before us. As he drew towards the end one piled up, one tingled in one's teeth. The last gesture, I have said, was to swing the arms out wide open, with the face held up. And when at last he swung out to this closing gesture I ceased even to breathe. It was ridiculous, of course, but you know that ghost-story feeling. It was after dinner, in a queer, old shadowy house. Would he, after all—?

There he stood for one stupendous moment, with his arms open and his upturned face, assured and bright, in the glare of the hanging lamp. We hung through that moment as if it were an age, and then came from all of us something that was half a sigh of infinite relief and half a reassuring "NO!" For visibly—he wasn't going. It was all nonsense. He had told an idle story, and carried it almost to conviction, that was all!... And then in that moment the face of Clayton, changed.

It changed. It changed as a lit house changes when its lights are suddenly extinguished. His eyes were suddenly eyes that were fixed, his smile was frozen on his lips, and he stood there still. He stood there, very gently swaying.

That moment, too, was an age. And then, you know, chairs were scraping, things were falling, and we were all moving. His knees seemed to give, and he fell forward, and Evans rose and caught him in his arms....

It stunned us all. For a minute I suppose no one said a coherent thing. We believed it, yet could not believe it.... I came out of a muddled stupefaction to find myself kneeling beside him, and his vest and shirt were torn open, and Sanderson's hand lay on his heart....

Well—the simple fact before us could very well wait our convenience; there was no hurry for us to comprehend. It lay there for an hour; it lies athwart my memory, black and amazing still, to this day. Clayton had, indeed, passed into the world that lies so near to and so far from our own, and he had gone thither by the only road that mortal man may take. But whether he did indeed pass there by that poor ghost's incantation, or whether he was stricken suddenly by apoplexy in the midst of an idle tale—as the coroner's jury would have us believe—is no matter for my judging; it is just one of those inexplicable riddles that must remain unsolved until the final solution of all things shall come. All I certainly know is that, in the very moment, in the very instant, of concluding those passes, he changed, and staggered, and fell down before us—dead!

7. JIMMY GOGGLES THE GOD

"It isn't every one who's been a god," said the sunburnt man. "But it's happened to me. Among other things."

I intimated my sense of his condescension.

"It don't leave much for ambition, does it?" said the sunburnt man.

"I was one of those men who were saved from the Ocean Pioneer. Gummy! how time flies! It's twenty years ago. I doubt if you'll remember anything of the Ocean Pioneer?"

The name was familiar, and I tried to recall when and where I had read it. The Ocean Pioneer? "Something about gold dust," I said vaguely, "but the precise—"

"That's it," he said. "In a beastly little channel she hadn't no business in—dodging pirates. It was before they'd put the kybosh on that business. And there'd been volcanoes or something and all the rocks was wrong. There's places about by Soona where you fair have to follow the rocks about to see where they're going next. Down she went in twenty fathoms before you could have dealt for whist, with fifty thousand pounds worth of gold aboard, it was said, in one form or another."

"Survivors?"

"Three."

"I remember the case now," I said. "There was something about salvage—"

But at the word salvage the sunburnt man exploded into language so extraordinarily horrible that I stopped aghast. He came down to more ordinary swearing, and pulled himself up abruptly. "Excuse me," he said, "but—salvage!"

He leant over towards me. "I was in that job," he said. "Tried to make myself a rich man, and got made a god instead. I've got my feelings—

"It ain't all jam being a god," said the sunburnt man, and for some time conversed by means of such pithy but unprogressive axioms. At last he took up his tale again.

"There was me," said the sunburnt man, "and a seaman named Jacobs, and Always, the mate of the Ocean Pioneer. And him it was that set the whole thing going. I remember him now, when we was in the jolly-boat, suggesting it all to our minds just by one sentence. He was a wonderful hand at suggesting things. 'There was forty thousand pounds,' he said, 'on that ship, and it's for me to say just where she went down.' It didn't need much brains to tumble to that. And he was the leader from the first to the last. He got hold of the Sanderses and their brig; they were brothers, and the brig was the Pride of Banya, and he it was bought the diving-dress—a second-hand one with a compressed air apparatus instead of pumping. He'd have done the diving too, if it hadn't made him sick going down. And the salvage people were mucking about with a chart he'd cooked up, as solemn as could be, at Starr Race, a hundred and twenty miles away.

"I can tell you we was a happy lot aboard that brig, jokes and drink and bright hopes all the time. It all seemed so neat and clean and straightforward, and what rough chaps call a 'cert.' And we used to speculate how the other blessed lot, the proper salvagers, who'd started two days before us, were getting on, until our sides fairly ached. We all messed together in the Sanderses' cabin—it was a curious crew, all officers and no men—and there stood the diving-dress waiting its turn. Young Sanders was a humorous sort of chap, and there certainly was something funny in the confounded thing's great fat head and its stare, and he made us see it too. 'Jimmie Goggles,' he used to call it, and talk to it like a Christian. Asked if he was married, and how Mrs. Goggles was, and all the little Goggleses. Fit to make you split. And every blessed day all of us used to drink the health of Jimmy Goggles in rum, and unscrew his eye and pour a glass of rum in him, until, instead of that nasty mackintosheriness, he smelt as nice in his inside as a cask of rum. It was jolly times we had in those days, I can tell you—little suspecting, poor chaps! what was a-coming.

"We weren't going to throw away our chances by any blessed hurry, you know, and we spent a whole day sounding our way towards where the Ocean Pioneer had gone down, right between two chunks of ropy grey rock—lava rocks that rose nearly out of the water. We had to lay off about half a mile to get a safe anchorage, and there was a thundering row who should stop on board. And there she lay just as she had gone down, so that you could see the top of the masts that was still standing perfectly distinctly. The row ending in all coming in the boat. I went down in the diving-dress on Friday morning directly it was light.

"What a surprise it was! I can see it all now quite distinctly. It was a queer-looking place, and the light was just coming. People over here think every blessed place in the tropics is a flat shore and palm trees and surf, bless 'em! This place, for instance, wasn't a bit that way. Not common rocks they were, undermined by waves; but great curved banks like ironwork cinder heaps, with green slime below, and thorny shrubs and things just waving upon them here and there, and the water glassy calm and clear, and showing you a kind of dirty grey-black shine, with huge flaring red-brown weeds spreading motionless, and crawling and darting things going through it. And far away beyond the ditches and pools and the heaps was a forest on the mountain flank, growing again after the fires and cinder showers of the last eruption. And the other way forest, too, and a kind of broken—what is it?—ambytheatre of black and rusty cinders rising out of it all, and the sea in a kind of bay in the middle.

"The dawn, I say, was just coming, and there wasn't much colour about things, and not a human being but ourselves anywhere in sight up or down the channel. Except the Pride of Banya, lying out beyond a lump of rocks towards the line of the sea.

"Not a human being in sight," he repeated, and paused.

"I don't know where they came from, not a bit. And we were feeling so safe that we were all alone that poor young Sanders was a-singing. I was in Jimmy Goggles, all except the helmet. 'Easy,' says Always, 'there's her mast.' And after I'd had just one squint over the gunwale, I caught up the bogey and almost tipped out as old Sanders brought the boat round. When the windows were screwed and everything was all right, I shut the valve from the air belt in order to help my sinking, and jumped overboard, feet foremost—for we hadn't a ladder. I left the boat pitching, and all of them staring down into the water after me, as my head sank down into the weeds and blackness that lay about the mast. I suppose nobody, not the most cautious chap in the world, would have bothered about a lookout at such a desolate place. It stunk of solitude.

"Of course you must understand that I was a greenhorn at diving. None of us were divers. We'd had to muck about with the thing to get the way of it, and this was the first time I'd been deep. It feels damnable. Your ears hurt beastly. I don't know if you've ever hurt yourself yawning or sneezing, but it takes you like that, only ten times worse. And a pain over the eyebrows here—splitting—and a feeling like influenza in the head. And it isn't all heaven in your lungs and things. And going down feels like the beginning of a lift, only it keeps on. And you can't turn your head to see what's above you, and you can't get a fair squint at what's happening to your feet without bending down something painful. And being deep it was dark, let alone the blackness of the ashes and mud that formed the bottom. It was like going down out of the dawn back into the night, so to speak.

"The mast came up like a ghost out of the black, and then a lot of fishes, and then a lot of flapping red seaweed, and then whack I came with a kind of dull bang on the deck of the Ocean Pioneer, and the fishes that had been feeding on the dead rose about me like a swarm of flies from road stuff in summer time. I turned on the compressed air again—for the suit was a bit thick and mackintoshery after all, in spite of the rum—and stood recovering myself. It struck coolish down there, and that helped take off the stuffiness a bit.

"When I began to feel easier, I started looking about me. It was an extraordinary sight. Even the light was extraordinary, a kind of reddy-coloured twilight, on account of the streamers of seaweed that floated up on either side of the ship. And far overhead just a moony, deep green-blue. The deck of the ship, except for a slight list to starboard, was level, and lay all dark and long between the weeds, clear except where the masts had snapped when she rolled, and vanishing into black night towards the forecastle. There wasn't any dead on the decks, most were in the weeds alongside, I suppose; but afterwards I found two skeletons lying in the passengers' cabins, where death had come to them. It was curious to stand on that deck and recognise it all, bit by bit; a place against the rail where I'd been fond of smoking by starlight, and the corner where an old chap from Sydney used to flirt with a widow we had aboard. A comfortable couple they'd been, only a month ago, and now you couldn't have got a meal for a baby crab off either of them.

"I've always had a bit of a philosophical turn, and I dare say I spent the best part of five minutes in such thoughts before I went below to find where the blessed dust was stored. It was slow work hunting, feeling it was for the most part, pitchy dark, with confusing blue gleams down the companion. And there were things moving about, a dab at my glass once, and once a pinch at my leg. Crabs, I expect. I kicked a lot of loose stuff that puzzled me, and stooped and picked up something all knobs and spikes. What do you think? Backbone! But I never had any particular feeling for bones. We had talked the affair over pretty thoroughly, and Always knew just where the stuff was stowed. I found it that trip. I lifted a box one end an inch or more."

He broke off in his story. "I've lifted it," he said, "as near as that! Forty thousand pounds worth of pure gold! Gold! I shouted inside my helmet as a kind of cheer and hurt my ears. I was getting confounded stuffy and tired by this time—I must have been down twenty-five minutes or more—and I thought this was good enough. I went up the companion again, and as my eyes came up flush with the deck, a thundering great crab gave a kind of hysterical jump and went scuttling off sideways. Quite a start it gave me. I stood up clear on deck and shut the valve behind the helmet to let the air accumulate to carry me up again—I noticed a kind of whacking from above, as though they were hitting the water with an oar, but I didn't look up. I fancied they were signalling me to come up.

"And then something shot down by me—something heavy, and stood a-quiver in the planks. I looked, and there was a long knife I'd seen young Sanders handling. Thinks I, he's dropped it, and I was still calling him this kind of fool and that—for it might have hurt me serious—when I began to lift and drive up towards the daylight. Just about the level of the top spars of the Ocean Pioneer, whack! I came against something sinking down, and a boot knocked in front of my helmet. Then something else, struggling frightful. It was a big weight atop of me, whatever it was, and moving and twisting about. I'd have thought it a big octopus, or some such thing, if it hadn't been for the boot. But octopuses don't wear boots. It was all in a moment, of course. I felt myself sinking down again, and I threw my arms about to keep steady, and the whole lot rolled free of me and shot down as I went up—"

He paused.

"I saw young Sanders's face, over a naked black shoulder, and a spear driven clean through his neck, and out of his mouth and neck what looked like spirts of pink smoke in the water. And down they went clutching one another, and turning over, and both too far gone to leave go. And in another second my helmet came a whack, fit to split, against the niggers' canoe. It was niggers! Two canoes full.

"It was lively times, I tell you! Overboard came Always with three spears in him. There was the legs of three or four black chaps kicking about me in the water. I couldn't see much, but I saw the game was up at a glance, gave my valve a tremendous twist, and went bubbling down again after poor Always, in as awful a state of scare and astonishment as you can well imagine. I passed young Sanders and the nigger going up again and struggling still a bit, and in another moment I was standing in the dim again on the deck of the Ocean Pioneer.

"'Gummy,' thinks I, 'here's a fix!' Niggers? At first I couldn't see anything for it but Stifle below or Stabs above. I didn't properly understand how much air there was to last me, but I didn't feel like standing very much more of it down below. I was hot and frightfully heady—quite apart from the blue funk I was in. We'd never repined with these beastly natives, filthy Papuan beasts. It wasn't any good, coming up where I was, but I had to do something. On the spur of the moment, I clambered over the side of the brig and landed among the weeds, and set off through the darkness as fast as I could. I just stopped once and knelt, and twisted back my head in the helmet and had a look up. It was a most extraordinary bright green-blue above, and the two canoes and the boat floating there very small and distant like a kind of twisted H. And it made me feel sick to squint up at it, and think what the pitching and swaying of the three meant.

"It was just about the most horrible ten minutes I ever had, blundering about in that darkness, pressure something awful, like being buried in sand, pain across the chest, sick with funk, and breathing nothing as it seemed but the smell of rum and mackintosh. Gummy! After a bit, I found myself going up a steepish sort of slope. I had another squint to see if anything was visible of the canoes and boats, and then kept on. I stopped with my head a foot from the surface, and tried to see where I was going, but, of course, nothing was to be seen but the reflection of the bottom. Then out I dashed like knocking my head through a mirror. Directly I got my eyes out of the water, I saw I'd come up a kind of beach near the forest. I had a look round, but the natives and the brig were both hidden by a big, hummucky heap of twisted lava, the born fool in me suggested a run for the woods. I didn't take the helmet off, but eased open one of the windows, and, after a bit of a pant, went on out of the water. You'd hardly imagine how clean and light the air tasted.

"Of course, with four inches of lead in your boot soles, and your head in a copper knob the size of a football, and been thirty-five minutes under water, you don't break any records running. I ran like a ploughboy going to work. And half way to the trees I saw a dozen niggers or more, coming out in a gaping, astonished sort of way to meet me.

"I just stopped dead, and cursed myself for all the fools out of London. I had about as much chance of cutting back to the water as a turned turtle. I just screwed up my window again to leave my hands free, and waited for them. There wasn't anything else for me to do.

"But they didn't come on very much. I began to suspect why. 'Jimmy Goggles,' I says, 'it's your beauty does it.' I was inclined to be a little light-headed, I think, with all these dangers about and the change in the pressure of the blessed air. 'Who're ye staring at?' I said, as if the savages could hear me. 'What d'ye take me for? I'm hanged if I don't give you something to stare at,' I said, and with that I screwed up the escape valve and turned on the compressed air from the belt, until I was swelled out like a blown frog. Regular imposing it must have been. I'm blessed if they'd come on a step; and presently one and then another went down on their hands and knees. They didn't know what to make of me, and they was doing the extra polite, which was very wise and reasonable of them. I had half a mind to edge back seaward and cut and run, but it seemed too hopeless. A step back and they'd have been after me. And out of sheer desperation I began to march towards them up the beach, with slow, heavy steps, and waving my blown-out arms about, in a dignified manner. And inside of me I was singing as small as a tomtit.

"But there's nothing like a striking appearance to help a man over a difficulty,—I've found that before and since. People like ourselves, who're up to diving-dresses by the time we're seven, can scarcely imagine the effect of one on a simple-minded savage. One or two of these niggers cut and run, the others started in a great hurry trying to knock their brains out on the ground. And on I went as slow and solemn and silly-looking and artful as a jobbing plumber. It was evident they took me for something immense.

"Then up jumped one and began pointing, making extraordinary gestures to me as he did so, and all the others began sharing their attention between me and something out at sea. 'What's the matter now?' I said. I turned slowly on account of my dignity, and there I saw, coming round a point, the poor old Pride of Banya towed by a couple of canoes. The sight fairly made me sick. But they evidently expected some recognition, so I waved my arms in a striking sort of non-committal manner. And then I turned and stalked on towards the trees again. At that time I was praying like mad, I remember, over and over again: 'Lord help me through with it! Lord help me through with it!' It's only fools who know nothing of dangers can afford to laugh at praying.

"But these niggers weren't going to let me walk through and away like that. They started a kind of bowing dance about me, and sort of pressed me to take a pathway that lay through the trees. It was clear to me they didn't take me for a British citizen, whatever else they thought of me, and for my own part I was never less anxious to own up to the old country.

"You'd hardly believe it, perhaps, unless you're familiar with savages, but these poor misguided, ignorant creatures took me straight to their kind of joss place to present me to the blessed old black stone there. By this time I was beginning to sort of realise the depth of their ignorance, and directly I set eyes on this deity I took my cue. I started a baritone howl, 'wow-wow,' very long on one note, and began waving my arms about a lot, and then very slowly and ceremoniously turned their image over on its side and sat down on it. I wanted to sit down badly, for diving-dresses ain't much wear in the tropics. Or, to put it different like, they're a sight too much. It took away their breath, I could see, my sitting on their joss, but in less time than a minute they made up their minds and were hard at work worshipping me. And I can tell you I felt a bit relieved to see things turning out so well, in spite of the weight on my shoulders and feet.

"But what made me anxious was what the chaps in the canoes might think when they came back. If they'd seen me in the boat before I went down, and without the helmet on—for they might have been spying and hiding since over night—they would very likely take a different view from the others. I was in a deuce of a stew about that for hours, as it seemed, until the shindy of the arrival began.

"But they took it down—the whole blessed village took it down. At the cost of sitting up stiff and stern, as much like those sitting Egyptian images one sees as I could manage, for pretty nearly twelve hours, I should guess at least, on end, I got over it. You'd hardly think what it meant in that heat and stink. I don't think any of them dreamt of the man inside. I was just a wonderful leathery great joss that had come up with luck out of the water. But the fatigue! the heat! the beastly closeness! the mackintosheriness and the rum! and the fuss! They lit a stinking fire on a kind of lava slab there was before me, and brought in a lot of gory muck—the worst parts of what they were feasting on outside, the Beasts—and burnt it all in my honour. I was getting a bit hungry, but I understand now how gods manage to do without eating, what with the smell of burnt offerings about them. And they brought in a lot of the stuff they'd got off the brig and, among other stuff, what I was a bit relieved to see, the kind of pneumatic pump that was used for the compressed air affair, and then a lot of chaps and girls came in and danced about me something disgraceful. It's extraordinary the different ways different people have of showing respect. If I'd had a hatchet handy I'd have gone for the lot of them—they made me feel that wild. All this time I sat as stiff as company, not knowing anything better to do. And at last, when nightfall came, and the wattle joss-house place got a bit too shadowy for their taste—all these here savages are afraid of the dark, you know—and I started a sort of 'Moo' noise, they built big bonfires outside and left me alone in peace in the darkness of my hut, free to unscrew my windows a bit and think things over, and feel just as bad as I liked. And, Lord! I was sick.

"I was weak and hungry, and my mind kept on behaving like a beetle on a pin, tremendous activity and nothing done at the end of it. Come round just where it was before. There was sorrowing for the other chaps, beastly drunkards certainly, but not deserving such a fate, and young Sanders with the spear through his neck wouldn't go out of my mind. There was the treasure down there in the Ocean Pioneer, and how one might get it and hide it somewhere safer, and get away and come back for it. And there was the puzzle where to get anything to eat. I tell you I was fair rambling. I was afraid to ask by signs for food, for fear of behaving too human, and so there I sat and hungered until very near the dawn. Then the village got a bit quiet, and I couldn't stand it any longer, and I went out and got some stuff like artichokes in a bowl and some sour milk. What was left of these I put away among the other offerings, just to give them a hint of my tastes. And in the morning they came to worship, and found me sitting up stiff and respectable on their previous god, just as they'd left me overnight. I'd got my back against the central pillar of the hut, and, practically, I was asleep. And that's how I became a god among the heathen—a false god no doubt, and blasphemous, but one can't always pick and choose.

"Now, I don't want to crack myself up as a god beyond my merits, but I must confess that while I was god to these people they was extraordinary successful. I don't say there's anything in it, mind you. They won a battle with another tribe—I got a lot of offerings I didn't want through it—they had wonderful fishing, and their crop of pourra was exceptional fine. And they counted the capture of the brig among the benefits I brought 'em. I must say I don't think that was a poor record for a perfectly new hand. And, though perhaps you'd scarcely credit it, I was the tribal god of those beastly savages for pretty nearly four months....

"What else could I do, man? But I didn't wear that diving-dress all the time. I made 'em rig me up a sort of holy of holies, and a deuce of a time I had too, making them understand what it was I wanted them to do. That indeed was the great difficulty—making them understand my wishes. I couldn't let myself down by talking their lingo badly—even if I'd been able to speak at all—and I couldn't go flapping a lot of gestures at them. So I drew pictures in sand and sat down beside them and hooted like one o'clock. Sometimes they did the things I wanted all right, and sometimes they did them all wrong. They was always very willing, certainly. All the while I was puzzling how I was to get the confounded business settled. Every night before the dawn I used to march out in full rig and go off to a place where I could see the channel in which the Ocean Pioneer lay sunk, and once even, one moonlight night, I tried to walk out to her, but the weeds and rocks and dark clean beat me. I didn't get back till full day, and then I found all those silly niggers out on the beach praying their sea-god to return to them. I was that vexed and tired, messing and tumbling about, and coming up and going down again, I could have punched their silly heads all round when they started rejoicing. I'm hanged if I like so much ceremony.

"And then came the missionary. That missionary! It was in the afternoon, and I was sitting in state in my outer temple place, sitting on that old black stone of theirs when he came. I heard a row outside and jabbering, and then his voice speaking to an interpreter. 'They worship stocks and stones,' he said, and I knew what was up, in a flash. I had one of my windows out for comfort, and I sang out straight away on the spur of the moment. 'Stocks and stones!' I says. 'You come inside,' I says, 'and I'll punch your blooming head.' There was a kind of silence and more jabbering, and in he came, Bible in hand, after the manner of them—a little sandy chap in specks and a pith helmet. I flatter myself that me sitting there in the shadows, with my copper head and my big goggles, struck him a bit of a heap at first. 'Well,' I says, 'how's the trade in calico?' for I don't hold with missionaries.

"I had a lark with that missionary. He was a raw hand, and quite outclassed with a man like me. He gasped out who was I, and I told him to read the inscription at my feet if he wanted to know. Down he goes to read, and his interpreter, being of course as superstitious as any of them, took it as an act of worship and plumped down like a shot. All my people gave a howl of triumph, and there wasn't any more business to be done in my village after that journey, not by the likes of him.

"But, of course, I was a fool to choke him off like that. If I'd had any sense I should have told him straight away of the treasure and taken him into Co.

I've no doubt he'd have come into Co. A child, with a few hours to think it over, could have seen the connection between my diving-dress and the loss of the Ocean Pioneer. A week after he left I went out one morning and saw the Motherhood, the salver's ship from Starr Race, towing up the channel and sounding. The whole blessed game was up, and all my trouble thrown away. Gummy! How wild I felt! And guying it in that stinking silly dress! Four months!"

The sunburnt man's story degenerated again. "Think of it," he said, when he emerged to linguistic purity once more. "Forty thousand pounds worth of gold."

"Did the little missionary come back?" I asked.

"Oh, yes! Bless him! And he pledged his reputation there was a man inside the god, and started out to see as much with tremendous ceremony. But there wasn't—he got sold again. I always did hate scenes and explanations, and long before he came I was out of it all—going home to Banya along the coast, hiding in bushes by day, and thieving food from the villages by night. Only weapon, a spear. No clothes, no money. Nothing. My face was my fortune, as the saying is. And just a squeak of eight thousand pounds of gold—fifth share. But the natives cut up rusty, thank goodness, because they thought it was him had driven their luck away."

8. THE NEW ACCELERATOR

Certainly, if ever a man found a guinea when he was looking for a pin it is my good friend Professor Gibberne. I have heard before of investigators overshooting the mark, but never quite to the extent that he has done. He has really, this time at any rate, without any touch of exaggeration in the phrase, found something to revolutionise human life. And that when he was simply seeking an all-round nervous stimulant to bring languid people up to the stresses of these pushful days. I have tasted the stuff now several times, and I cannot do better than describe the effect the thing had on me. That there are astonishing experiences in store for all in search of new sensations will become apparent enough.

Professor Gibberne, as many people know, is my neighbour in Folkestone. Unless my memory plays me a trick, his portrait at various ages has already appeared in The Strand Magazine—I think late in 1899; but I am unable to look it up because I have lent that volume to some one who has never sent it back. The reader may, perhaps, recall the high forehead and the singularly long black eyebrows that give such a Mephistophelian touch to his face. He occupies one of those pleasant little detached houses in the mixed style that make the western end of the Upper Sandgate Road so interesting. His is the one with the Flemish gables and the Moorish portico, and it is in the little room with the mullioned bay window that he works when he is down here, and in which of an evening we have so often smoked and talked together. He is a mighty jester, but, besides, he likes to talk to me about his work; he is one of those men who find a help and stimulus in talking, and so I have been able to follow the conception of the New Accelerator right up from a very early stage. Of course, the greater portion of his experimental work is not done in Folkestone, but in Gower Street, in the fine new laboratory next to the hospital that he has been the first to use.

As every one knows, or at least as all intelligent people know, the special department in which Gibberne has gained so great and deserved a reputation among physiologists is the action of drugs upon the nervous system. Upon soporifics, sedatives, and anaesthetics he is, I am told, unequalled. He is also a chemist of considerable eminence, and I suppose in the subtle and complex jungle of riddles that centres about the ganglion cell and the axis fibre there are little cleared places of his making, little glades of illumination, that, until he sees fit to publish his results, are still inaccessible to every other living man. And in the last few years he has been particularly assiduous upon this question of nervous stimulants, and already, before the discovery of the New Accelerator, very successful with them. Medical science has to thank him for at least three distinct and absolutely safe invigorators of unrivalled value to practising men. In cases of exhaustion the preparation known as Gibberne's

B Syrup has, I suppose, saved more lives already than any lifeboat round the coast.

"But none of these little things begin to satisfy me yet," he told me nearly a year ago. "Either they increase the central energy without affecting the nerves or they simply increase the available energy by lowering the nervous conductivity; and all of them are unequal and local in their operation. One wakes up the heart and viscera and leaves the brain stupefied, one gets at the brain champagne fashion and does nothing good for the solar plexus, and what I want—and what, if it's an earthly possibility, I mean to have—is a stimulant that stimulates all round, that wakes you up for a time from the crown of your head to the tip of your great toe, and makes you go two—or even three—to everybody else's one. Eh? That's the thing I'm after."

"It would tire a man," I said.

"Not a doubt of it. And you'd eat double or treble—and all that. But just think what the thing would mean. Imagine yourself with a little phial like this"—he held up a little bottle of green glass and marked his points with it—"and in this precious phial is the power to think twice as fast, move twice as quickly, do twice as much work in a given time as you could otherwise do."

"But is such a thing possible?"

"I believe so. If it isn't, I've wasted my time for a year. These various preparations of the hypophosphites, for example, seem to show that something of the sort... Even if it was only one and a half times as fast it would do."

"It WOULD do," I said.

"If you were a statesman in a corner, for example, time rushing up against you, something urgent to be done, eh?"

"He could dose his private secretary," I said.

"And gain—double time. And think if YOU, for example, wanted to finish a book."

"Usually," I said, "I wish I'd never begun 'em."

"Or a doctor, driven to death, wants to sit down and think out a case. Or a barrister—or a man cramming for an examination."

"Worth a guinea a drop," said I, "and more to men like that."

"And in a duel, again," said Gibberne, "where it all depends on your quickness in pulling the trigger."

"Or in fencing," I echoed.

"You see," said Gibberne, "if I get it as an all-round thing it will really do you no harm at all—except perhaps to an infinitesimal degree it brings you nearer old age. You will just have lived twice to other people's once—"

"I suppose," I meditated, "in a duel—it would be fair?"

"That's a question for the seconds," said Gibberne.

I harked back further. "And you really think such a thing IS possible?" I said.

"As possible," said Gibberne, and glanced at something that went throbbing by the window, "as a motor-bus. As a matter of fact—"

He paused and smiled at me deeply, and tapped slowly on the edge of his desk with the green phial. "I think I know the stuff.... Already I've got something coming." The nervous smile upon his face betrayed the gravity of his revelation. He rarely talked of his actual experimental work unless things were very near the end. "And it may be, it may be—I shouldn't be surprised—it may even do the thing at a greater rate than twice."

"It will be rather a big thing," I hazarded.

"It will be, I think, rather a big thing."

But I don't think he quite knew what a big thing it was to be, for all that.

I remember we had several talks about the stuff after that. "The New Accelerator" he called it, and his tone about it grew more confident on each occasion. Sometimes he talked nervously of unexpected physiological results its use might have, and then he would get a little unhappy; at others he was frankly mercenary, and we debated long and anxiously how the preparation might be turned to commercial account. "It's a good thing," said Gibberne, "a tremendous thing. I know I'm giving the world something, and I think it only reasonable we should expect the world to pay. The dignity of science is all very well, but I think somehow I must have the monopoly of the stuff for, say, ten years. I don't see why ALL the fun in life should go to the dealers in ham."

My own interest in the coming drug certainly did not wane in the time. I have always had a queer little twist towards metaphysics in my mind. I have always been given to paradoxes about space and time, and it seemed to me that Gibberne was really preparing no less than the absolute acceleration of life. Suppose a man repeatedly dosed with such a preparation: he would live an active and record life indeed, but he would be an adult at eleven, middle-aged at twenty-five, and by thirty well on the road to senile decay. It seemed to me that so far Gibberne was only going to do for any one who took his drug exactly what Nature has done for the Jews and Orientals, who are men in their teens and aged by fifty, and quicker in thought and act than we are all the time. The marvel of drugs has always been great to my mind; you can madden a man, calm a man, make him incredibly strong and alert or a helpless log, quicken this passion and allay that, all by means of drugs, and here was a new miracle to be added to this strange armoury of phials the doctors use! But Gibberne was far too eager upon his technical points to enter very keenly into my aspect of the question.

It was the 7th or 8th of August when he told me the distillation that would decide his failure or success for a time was going forward as we talked, and it was on the 10th that he told me the thing was done and the New Accelerator a tangible reality in the world. I met him as I was going up the Sandgate Hill towards Folkestone—I think I was going to get my hair cut, and he came hurrying down to meet me—I suppose he was coming to my house to tell me at once of his success. I remember that his eyes were unusually bright and his face flushed, and I noted even then the swift alacrity of his step.

"It's done," he cried, and gripped my hand, speaking very fast; "it's more than done. Come up to my house and see."

"Really?"

"Really!" he shouted. "Incredibly! Come up and see."

"And it does—twice?"

"It does more, much more. It scares me. Come up and see the stuff. Taste it! Try it! It's the most amazing stuff on earth." He gripped my arm and, walking at such a pace that he forced me into a trot, went shouting with me up the hill. A whole char-a-banc-ful of people turned and stared at us in unison after the manner of people in chars-a-banc. It was one of those hot, clear days that Folkestone sees so much of, every colour incredibly bright and every outline hard. There was a breeze, of course, but not so much breeze as sufficed under these conditions to keep me cool and dry. I panted for mercy.

"I'm not walking fast, am I?" cried Gibberne, and slackened his pace to a quick march.

"You've been taking some of this stuff," I puffed.

"No," he said. "At the utmost a drop of water that stood in a beaker from which I had washed out the last traces of the stuff. I took some last night, you know. But that is ancient history, now."

"And it goes twice?" I said, nearing his doorway in a grateful perspiration.

"It goes a thousand times, many thousand times!" cried Gibberne, with a dramatic gesture, flinging open his Early English carved oak gate.

"Phew!" said I, and followed him to the door.

"I don't know how many times it goes," he said, with his latch-key in his hand.

"And you—"

"It throws all sorts of light on nervous physiology, it kicks the theory of vision into a perfectly new shape!... Heaven knows how many thousand times. We'll try all that after—The thing is to try the stuff now."

"Try the stuff?" I said, as we went along the passage.

"Rather," said Gibberne, turning on me in his study. "There it is in that little green phial there! Unless you happen to be afraid?"

I am a careful man by nature, and only theoretically adventurous. I WAS afraid. But on the other hand there is pride.

"Well," I haggled. "You say you've tried it?"

"I've tried it," he said, "and I don't look hurt by it, do I? I don't even look livery and I FEEL—"

I sat down. "Give me the potion," I said. "If the worst comes to the worst it will save having my hair cut, and that I think is one of the most hateful duties of a civilised man. How do you take the mixture?"

"With water," said Gibberne, whacking down a carafe.

He stood up in front of his desk and regarded me in his easy chair; his manner was suddenly affected by a touch of the Harley Street specialist. "It's rum stuff, you know," he said.

I made a gesture with my hand.

"I must warn you in the first place as soon as you've got it down to shut your eyes, and open them very cautiously in a minute or so's time. One still sees. The sense of vision is a question of length of vibration, and not of multitude of impacts; but there's a kind of shock to the retina, a nasty giddy confusion just at the time, if the eyes are open. Keep 'em shut."

"Shut," I said. "Good!"

"And the next thing is, keep still. Don't begin to whack about. You may fetch something a nasty rap if you do. Remember you will be going several thousand times faster than you ever did before, heart, lungs, muscles, brain—everything—and you will hit hard without knowing it. You won't know it, you know. You'll feel just as you do now. Only everything in the world will seem to be going ever so many thousand times slower than it ever went before. That's what makes it so deuced queer."

"Lor'," I said. "And you mean—"

"You'll see," said he, and took up a little measure. He glanced at the material on his desk. "Glasses," he said, "water. All here. Mustn't take too much for the first attempt."

The little phial glucked out its precious contents.

"Don't forget what I told you," he said, turning the contents of the measure into a glass in the manner of an Italian waiter measuring whisky. "Sit with the eyes tightly shut and in absolute stillness for two minutes," he said. "Then you will hear me speak."

He added an inch or so of water to the little dose in each glass.

"By-the-by," he said, "don't put your glass down. Keep it in your hand and rest your hand on your knee. Yes—so. And now—"

He raised his glass.

"The New Accelerator," I said.

"The New Accelerator," he answered, and we touched glasses and drank, and instantly I closed my eyes.

You know that blank non-existence into which one drops when one has taken "gas." For an indefinite interval it was like that. Then I heard Gibberne telling me to wake up, and I stirred and opened my eyes. There he stood as he had been standing, glass still in hand. It was empty, that was all the difference.

"Well?" said I.

"Nothing out of the way?"

"Nothing. A slight feeling of exhilaration, perhaps. Nothing more."

"Sounds?"

"Things are still," I said. "By Jove! yes! They ARE still. Except the sort of faint pat, patter, like rain falling on different things. What is it?"

"Analysed sounds," I think he said, but I am not sure. He glanced at the window. "Have you ever seen a curtain before a window fixed in that way before?"

I followed his eyes, and there was the end of the curtain, frozen, as it were, corner high, in the act of flapping briskly in the breeze.

"No," said I; "that's odd."

"And here," he said, and opened the hand that held the glass. Naturally I winced, expecting the glass to smash. But so far from smashing it did not even seem to stir; it hung in mid-air—motionless.

"Roughly speaking," said Gibberne, "an object in these latitudes falls 16 feet in the first second. This glass is falling 16 feet in a second now. Only, you see, it hasn't been falling yet for the hundredth part of a second. That gives you some idea of the pace of my Accelerator." And he waved his hand round and round, over and under the slowly sinking glass. Finally, he took it by the bottom, pulled it down, and placed it very carefully on the table. "Eh?" he said to me, and laughed.

"That seems all right," I said, and began very gingerly to raise myself from my chair. I felt perfectly well, very light and comfortable, and quite confident in my mind. I was going fast all over. My heart, for example, was beating a thousand times a second, but that caused me no discomfort at all. I looked out of the window. An immovable cyclist, head down and with a frozen puff of dust behind his driving-wheel, scorched to overtake a galloping char-a-banc that did not stir. I gaped in amazement at this incredible spectacle. "Gibberne," I cried, "how long will this confounded stuff last?"

"Heaven knows!" he answered. "Last time I took it I went to bed and slept it off. I tell you, I was frightened. It must have lasted some minutes, I think—it seemed like hours. But after a bit it slows down rather suddenly, I believe."

I was proud to observe that I did not feel frightened—I suppose because there were two of us. "Why shouldn't we go out?" I asked.

"Why not?"

"They'll see us."

"Not they. Goodness, no! Why, we shall be going a thousand times faster than the quickest conjuring trick that was ever done. Come along! Which way shall we go? Window, or door?"

And out by the window we went.

Assuredly of all the strange experiences that I have ever had, or imagined, or read of other people having or imagining, that little raid I made with Gibberne on the Folkestone Leas, under the influence of the New Accelerator, was the strangest and maddest of all. We went out by his gate into the road, and there we made a minute examination of the statuesque passing traffic. The tops of the wheels and some of the legs of the horses of this char-a-banc, the end of the whip-lash and the lower jaw of the conductor—who was just beginning to yawn—were perceptibly in motion, but all the rest of the lumbering conveyance seemed still. And quite noiseless except for a faint rattling that came from one man's throat! And as parts of this frozen edifice there were a driver, you know, and a conductor, and eleven people! The effect as we walked about the thing began by being madly queer, and ended by being disagreeable. There they were, people like ourselves and yet not like ourselves, frozen in careless attitudes, caught in mid-gesture. A girl and a man smiled at one another, a leering smile that threatened to last for evermore; a woman in a floppy capelline rested her arm on the rail and stared at Gibberne's house with the unwinking stare of eternity; a man stroked his moustache like a figure of wax, and another stretched a tiresome stiff hand with extended fingers towards his loosened hat. We stared at them, we laughed at them, we made faces at them, and then a sort of disgust of them came upon us, and we turned away and walked round in front of the cyclist towards the Leas.

"Goodness!" cried Gibberne, suddenly; "look there!"

He pointed, and there at the tip of his finger and sliding down the air with wings flapping slowly and at the speed of an exceptionally languid snail—was a bee.

And so we came out upon the Leas. There the thing seemed madder than ever. The band was playing in the upper stand, though all the sound it made for us was a low-pitched, wheezy rattle, a sort of prolonged last sigh that passed at times into a sound like the slow, muffled ticking of some monstrous clock. Frozen people stood erect, strange, silent, self-conscious-looking dummies hung unstably in mid-stride, promenading upon the grass. I passed close to a little poodle dog suspended in the act of leaping, and watched the slow movement of his legs as he sank to earth. "Lord, look here!" cried Gibberne, and we halted for a moment before a magnificent person in white faint-striped flannels, white shoes, and a Panama hat, who turned back to wink at two gaily dressed ladies he had passed. A wink, studied with such leisurely deliberation as we could afford, is an unattractive thing. It loses any quality of alert gaiety, and one remarks that the winking eye does not completely close, that under its drooping lid appears the lower edge of an eyeball and a little line of white. "Heaven give me memory," said I, "and I will never wink again."

"Or smile," said Gibberne, with his eye on the lady's answering teeth.

"It's infernally hot, somehow," said I. "Let's go slower."

"Oh, come along!" said Gibberne.

We picked our way among the bath-chairs in the path. Many of the people sitting in the chairs seemed almost natural in their passive poses, but the contorted scarlet of the bandsmen was not a restful thing to see. A purple-faced little gentleman was frozen in the midst of a violent struggle to refold his newspaper against the wind; there were many evidences that all these people in their sluggish way were exposed to a considerable breeze, a breeze that had no existence so far as our sensations went. We came out and walked a little way from the crowd, and turned and regarded it. To see all that multitude changed, to a picture, smitten rigid, as it were, into the semblance of realistic wax, was impossibly wonderful. It was absurd, of course; but it filled me with an irrational, an exultant sense of superior advantage. Consider the wonder of it! All that I had said, and thought, and done since the stuff had begun to work in my veins had happened, so far as those people, so far as the world in general went, in the twinkling of an eye. "The New Accelerator—" I began, but Gibberne interrupted me.

"There's that infernal old woman!" he said.

"What old woman?"

"Lives next door to me," said Gibberne. "Has a lapdog that yaps. Gods! The temptation is strong!"

There is something very boyish and impulsive about Gibberne at times. Before I could expostulate with him he had dashed forward, snatched the unfortunate animal out of visible existence, and was running violently with it towards the cliff of the Leas. It was most extraordinary. The little brute, you know, didn't bark or wriggle or make the slightest sign of vitality. It kept quite stiffly in an attitude of somnolent repose, and Gibberne held it by the neck. It was like running about with a dog of wood. "Gibberne," I cried, "put it down!" Then I said something else. "If you run like that, Gibberne," I cried, "you'll set your clothes on fire. Your linen trousers are going brown as it is!"

He clapped his hand on his thigh and stood hesitating on the verge. "Gibberne," I cried, coming up, "put it down. This heat is too much! It's our running so! Two or three miles a second! Friction of the air!"

"What?" he said, glancing at the dog.

"Friction of the air," I shouted. "Friction of the air. Going too fast. Like meteorites and things. Too hot. And, Gibberne! Gibberne! I'm all over pricking and a sort of perspiration. You can see people stirring slightly. I believe the stuff's working off! Put that dog down."

"Eh?" he said.

"It's working off," I repeated. "We're too hot and the stuff's working off! I'm wet through."

He stared at me. Then at the band, the wheezy rattle of whose performance was certainly going faster. Then with a tremendous sweep of the arm he hurled the dog away from him and it went spinning upward, still inanimate, and hung at last over the grouped parasols of a knot of chattering people.

Gibberne was gripping my elbow. "By Jove!" he cried. "I believe—it is! A sort of hot pricking and—yes. That man's moving his pocket-handkerchief! Perceptibly. We must get out of this sharp."

But we could not get out of it sharply enough. Luckily, perhaps! For we might have run, and if we had run we should, I believe, have burst into flames. Almost certainly we should have burst into flames! You know we had neither of us thought of that.... But before we could even begin to run the action of the drug had ceased. It was the business of a minute fraction of a second. The effect of the New Accelerator passed like the drawing of a curtain, vanished in the movement of a hand. I heard Gibberne's voice in infinite alarm. "Sit down," he said, and flop, down upon the turf at the edge of the Leas I sat—scorching as I sat. There is a patch of burnt grass there still where I sat down. The whole stagnation seemed to wake up as I did so, the disarticulated vibration of the band rushed together into a blast of music, the promenaders put their feet down and walked their ways, the papers and flags began flapping, smiles passed into words, the winker finished his wink and went on his way complacently, and all the seated people moved and spoke.

The whole world had come alive again, was going as fast as we were, or rather we were going no faster than the rest of the world. It was like slowing down as one comes into a railway station. Everything seemed to spin round for a second or two, I had the most transient feeling of nausea, and that was all. And the little dog which had seemed to hang for a moment when the force of Gibberne's arm was expended fell with a swift acceleration clean through a lady's parasol!

That was the saving of us. Unless it was for one corpulent old gentleman in a bath-chair, who certainly did start at the sight of us and afterwards regarded us at intervals with a darkly suspicious eye, and, finally, I believe, said something to his nurse about us, I doubt if a solitary person remarked our sudden appearance among them. Plop! We must have appeared abruptly. We ceased to smoulder almost at once, though the turf beneath me was uncomfortably hot. The attention of every one—including even the Amusements' Association band, which on this occasion, for the only time in its history, got out of tune—was arrested by the amazing fact, and the still more amazing yapping and uproar caused by the fact that a respectable, over-fed lap-dog sleeping quietly to the east of the bandstand should suddenly fall through the parasol of a lady on the west—in a slightly singed condition due to the extreme velocity of its movements through the air. In these absurd days, too, when we are all trying to be as psychic, and silly, and superstitious as possible! People got up and trod on other people, chairs were overturned, the Leas policeman ran. How the matter settled itself I do not know—we were much too anxious to disentangle ourselves from the affair and get out of range of the eye of the old gentleman in the bath-chair to make minute inquiries. As soon as we were sufficiently cool and sufficiently recovered from our giddiness and nausea and confusion of mind to do so we stood up and, skirting the crowd, directed our steps back along the road below the Metropole towards Gibberne's house. But amidst the din I heard very distinctly the gentleman who had been sitting beside the lady of the ruptured sunshade using quite unjustifiable threats and language to one of those chair-attendants who have "Inspector" written on their caps. "If you didn't throw the dog," he said, "who DID?"

The sudden return of movement and familiar noises, and our natural anxiety about ourselves (our clothe's were still dreadfully hot, and the fronts of the thighs of Gibberne's white trousers were scorched a drabbish brown), prevented the minute observations I should have liked to make on all these things. Indeed, I really made no observations of any scientific value on that return. The bee, of course, had gone. I looked for that cyclist, but he was already out of sight as we came into the Upper Sandgate Road or hidden from us by traffic; the char-a-banc, however, with its people now all alive and stirring, was clattering along at a spanking pace almost abreast of the nearer church.

We noted, however, that the window-sill on which we had stepped in getting out of the house was slightly singed, and that the impressions of our feet on the gravel of the path were unusually deep.

So it was I had my first experience of the New Accelerator. Practically we had been running about and saying and doing all sorts of things in the space of a second or so of time. We had lived half an hour while the band had played, perhaps, two bars. But the effect it had upon us was that the whole world had stopped for our convenient inspection. Considering all things, and particularly considering our rashness in venturing out of the house, the experience might certainly have been much more disagreeable than it was. It showed, no doubt, that Gibberne has still much to learn before his preparation is a manageable convenience, but its practicability it certainly demonstrated beyond all cavil.

Since that adventure he has been steadily bringing its use under control, and I have several times, and without the slightest bad result, taken measured doses under his direction; though I must confess I have not yet ventured abroad again while under its influence. I may mention, for example, that this story has been written at one sitting and without interruption, except for the nibbling of some chocolate, by its means. I began at 6.25, and my watch is now very nearly at the minute past the half-hour. The convenience of securing a long, uninterrupted spell of work in the midst of a day full of engagements cannot be exaggerated. Gibberne is now working at the quantitative handling of his preparation, with especial reference to its distinctive effects upon different types of constitution. He then hopes to find a Retarder with which to dilute its present rather excessive potency. The Retarder will, of course, have the reverse effect to the Accelerator; used alone it should enable the patient to spread a few seconds over many hours of ordinary time,—and so to maintain an apathetic inaction, a glacier-like absence of alacrity, amidst the most animated or irritating surroundings. The two things together must necessarily work an entire revolution in civilised existence. It is the beginning of our escape from that Time Garment of which Carlyle speaks. While this Accelerator will enable us to concentrate ourselves with tremendous impact upon any moment or occasion that demands our utmost sense and vigour, the Retarder will enable us to pass in passive tranquillity through infinite hardship and tedium. Perhaps I am a little optimistic about the Retarder, which has indeed still to be discovered, but about the Accelerator there is no possible sort of doubt whatever. Its appearance upon the market in a convenient, controllable, and assimilable form is a matter of the next few months. It will be obtainable of all chemists and druggists, in small green bottles, at a high but, considering its extraordinary qualities, by no means excessive price. Gibberne's Nervous Accelerator it will be called, and he hopes to be able to supply it in three strengths: one in 200, one in 900, and one in 2000, distinguished by yellow, pink, and white labels respectively.

No doubt its use renders a great number of very extraordinary things possible; for, of course, the most remarkable and, possibly, even criminal proceedings may be effected with impunity by thus dodging, as it were, into the interstices of time. Like all potent preparations it will be liable to abuse. We have, however, discussed this aspect of the question very thoroughly, and we have decided that this is purely a matter of medical jurisprudence and altogether outside our province. We shall manufacture and sell the Accelerator, and, as for the consequences—we shall see.

9. MR. LEDBETTER'S VACATION

My friend, Mr. Ledbetter, is a round-faced little man, whose natural mildness of eye is gigantically exaggerated when you catch the beam through his glasses, and whose deep, deliberate voice irritates irritable people. A certain elaborate clearness of enunciation has come with him to his present vicarage from his scholastic days, an elaborate clearness of enunciation and a certain nervous determination to be firm and correct upon all issues, important and unimportant alike. He is a sacerdotalist and a chess player, and suspected by many of the secret practice of the higher mathematics—creditable rather than interesting things. His conversation is copious and given much to needless detail. By many, indeed, his intercourse is condemned, to put it plainly, as "boring," and such have even done me the compliment to wonder why I countenance him. But, on the other hand, there is a large faction who marvel at his countenancing such a dishevelled, discreditable acquaintance as myself. Few appear to regard our friendship with equanimity. But that is because they do not know of the link that binds us, of my amiable connection via Jamaica with Mr. Ledbetter's past.

About that past he displays an anxious modesty. "I do not KNOW what I should do if it became known," he says; and repeats, impressively, "I do not know WHAT I should do." As a matter of fact, I doubt if he would do anything except get very red about the ears. But that will appear later; nor will I tell here of our first encounter, since, as a general rule—though I am prone to break it—the end of a story should come after, rather than before, the beginning. And the beginning of the story goes a long way back; indeed, it is now nearly twenty years since Fate, by a series of complicated and startling manoeuvres, brought Mr. Ledbetter, so to speak, into my hands.

In those days I was living in Jamaica, and Mr. Ledbetter was a schoolmaster in England. He was in orders, and already recognisably the same man that he is to-day: the same rotundity of visage, the same or similar glasses, and the same faint shadow of surprise in his resting expression. He was, of course, dishevelled when I saw him, and his collar less of a collar than a wet bandage, and that may have helped to bridge the natural gulf between us—but of that, as I say, later.

The business began at Hithergate-on-Sea, and simultaneously with Mr. Ledbetter's summer vacation. Thither he came for a greatly needed rest, with a bright brown portmanteau marked "F. W. L.", a new white-and-black straw hat, and two pairs of white flannel trousers. He was naturally exhilarated at his release from school—for he was not very fond of the boys he taught. After dinner he fell into a discussion with a talkative person established in the boarding-house to which, acting on the advice of his aunt, he had resorted. This talkative person was the only other man in the house. Their discussion concerned the melancholy disappearance of wonder and adventure in these latter days, the prevalence of globe-trotting, the abolition of distance by steam and electricity, the vulgarity of advertisement, the degradation of men by civilisation, and many such things. Particularly was the talkative person eloquent on the decay of human courage through security, a security Mr. Ledbetter rather thoughtlessly joined him in deploring. Mr. Ledbetter, in the first delight of emancipation from "duty," and being anxious, perhaps, to establish a reputation for manly conviviality, partook, rather more freely than was advisable, of the excellent whisky the talkative person produced. But he did not become intoxicated, he insists.

He was simply eloquent beyond his sober wont, and with the finer edge gone from his judgment. And after that long talk of the brave old days that were past forever, he went out into moonlit Hithergate—alone and up the cliff road where the villas cluster together.

He had bewailed, and now as he walked up the silent road he still bewailed, the fate that had called him to such an uneventful life as a pedagogue's. What a prosaic existence he led, so stagnant, so colourless! Secure, methodical, year in year out, what call was there for bravery? He thought enviously of those roving, mediaeval days, so near and so remote, of quests and spies and condottieri and many a risky blade-drawing business. And suddenly came a doubt, a strange doubt, springing out of some chance thought of tortures, and destructive altogether of the position he had assumed that evening.

Was he—Mr. Ledbetter—really, after all, so brave as he assumed? Would he really be so pleased to have railways, policemen, and security vanish suddenly from the earth?

The talkative man had spoken enviously of crime. "The burglar," he said, "is the only true adventurer left on earth. Think of his single-handed fight against the whole civilised world!" And Mr. Ledbetter had echoed his envy. "They DO have some fun out of life," Mr. Ledbetter had said. "And about the only people who do. Just think how it must feel to wire a lawn!" And he had laughed wickedly. Now, in this franker intimacy of self-communion he found himself instituting a comparison between his own brand of courage and that of the habitual criminal. He tried to meet these insidious questionings with blank assertion. "I could do all that," said Mr. Ledbetter. "I long to do all that. Only I do not give way to my criminal impulses. My moral courage restrains me." But he doubted even while he told himself these things.

Mr. Ledbetter passed a large villa standing by itself. Conveniently situated above a quiet, practicable balcony was a window, gaping black, wide open. At the time he scarcely marked it, but the picture of it came with him, wove into his thoughts. He figured himself climbing up that balcony, crouching—

plunging into that dark, mysterious interior. "Bah! You would not dare," said the Spirit of Doubt. "My duty to my fellow-men forbids," said Mr. Ledbetter's self-respect.

It was nearly eleven, and the little seaside town was already very still. The whole world slumbered under the moonlight. Only one warm oblong of window-blind far down the road spoke of waking life. He turned and came back slowly towards the villa of the open window. He stood for a time outside the gate, a battlefield of motives. "Let us put things to the test," said Doubt. "For the satisfaction of these intolerable doubts, show that you dare go into that house. Commit a burglary in blank. That, at any rate, is no crime." Very softly he opened and shut the gate and slipped into the shadow of the shrubbery. "This is foolish," said Mr. Ledbetter's caution. "I expected that," said Doubt. His heart was beating fast, but he was certainly not afraid. He was NOT afraid. He remained in that shadow for some considerable time.

The ascent of the balcony, it was evident, would have to be done in a rush, for it was all in clear moonlight, and visible from the gate into the avenue. A trellis thinly set with young, ambitious climbing roses made the ascent ridiculously easy. There, in that black shadow by the stone vase of flowers, one might crouch and take a closer view of this gaping breach in the domestic defences, the open window. For a while Mr. Ledbetter was as still as the night, and then that insidious whisky tipped the balance. He dashed forward. He went up the trellis with quick, convulsive movements, swung his legs over the parapet of the balcony, and dropped panting in the shadow even as he had designed. He was trembling violently, short of breath, and his heart pumped noisily, but his mood was exultation. He could have shouted to find he was so little afraid.

A happy line that he had learnt from Wills's "Mephistopheles" came into his mind as he crouched there. "I feel like a cat on the tiles," he whispered to himself. It was far better than he had expected—this adventurous exhilaration. He was sorry for all poor men to whom burglary was unknown. Nothing happened. He was quite safe. And he was acting in the bravest manner!

And now for the window, to make the burglary complete! Must he dare do that? Its position above the front door defined it as a landing or passage, and there were no looking-glasses or any bedroom signs about it, or any other window on the first floor, to suggest the possibility of a sleeper within. For a time he listened under the ledge, then raised his eyes above the sill and peered in. Close at hand, on a pedestal, and a little startling at first, was a nearly life-size gesticulating bronze. He ducked, and after some time he peered again. Beyond was a broad landing, faintly gleaming; a flimsy fabric of bead curtain, very black and sharp, against a further window; a broad staircase, plunging into a gulf of darkness below; and another ascending to the second floor. He glanced behind him, but the stillness of the night was unbroken. "Crime," he whispered, "crime," and scrambled softly and swiftly over the sill into the house. His feet fell noiselessly on a mat of skin. He was a burglar indeed!

He crouched for a time, all ears and peering eyes. Outside was a scampering and rustling, and for a moment he repented of his enterprise. A short "miaow," a spitting, and a rush into silence, spoke reassuringly of cats. His courage grew. He stood up. Every one was abed, it seemed. So easy is it to commit a burglary, if one is so minded. He was glad he had put it to the test. He determined to take some petty trophy, just to prove his freedom from any abject fear of the law, and depart the way he had come.

He peered about him, and suddenly the critical spirit arose again. Burglars did far more than such mere elementary entrance as this: they went into rooms, they forced safes. Well—he was not afraid. He could not force safes, because that would be a stupid want of consideration for his hosts. But he would go into rooms—he would go upstairs. More: he told himself that he was perfectly secure; an empty house could not be more reassuringly still. He had to clench his hands, nevertheless, and summon all his resolution before he began very softly to ascend the dim staircase, pausing for several seconds between each step. Above was a square landing with one open and several closed doors; and all the house was still. For a moment he stood wondering what would happen if some sleeper woke suddenly and emerged. The open door showed a moonlit bedroom, the coverlet white and undisturbed. Into this room he crept in three interminable minutes and took a piece of soap for his plunder—his trophy. He turned to descend even more softly than he had ascended. It was as easy as—

Hist!...

Footsteps! On the gravel outside the house—and then the noise of a latchkey, the yawn and bang of a door, and the spitting of a match in the hall below. Mr. Ledbetter stood petrified by the sudden discovery of the folly upon which he had come. "How on earth am I to get out of this?" said Mr. Ledbetter.

The hall grew bright with a candle flame, some heavy object bumped against the umbrella-stand, and feet were ascending the staircase. In a flash Mr. Ledbetter realised that his retreat was closed. He stood for a moment, a pitiful figure of penitent confusion. "My goodness! What a FOOL I have been!" he whispered, and then darted swiftly across the shadowy landing into the empty bedroom from which he had just come. He stood listening—quivering. The footsteps reached the first-floor landing.

Horrible thought! This was possibly the latecomer's room! Not a moment was to be lost! Mr. Ledbetter stooped beside the bed, thanked Heaven for a valance, and crawled within its protection not ten seconds too soon. He became motionless on hands and knees. The advancing candle-light appeared through the thinner stitches of the fabric, the shadows ran wildly about, and became rigid as the candle was put down.

"Lord, what a day!" said the newcomer, blowing noisily, and it seemed he deposited some heavy burthen on what Mr. Ledbetter, judging by the feet, decided to be a writing-table. The unseen then went to the door and locked it, examined the fastenings of the windows carefully and pulled down the blinds, and returning sat down upon the bed with startling ponderosity.

"WHAT a day!" he said. "Good Lord!" and blew again, and Mr. Ledbetter inclined to believe that the person was mopping his face. His boots were good stout boots; the shadows of his legs upon the valance suggested a formidable stoutness of aspect. After a time he removed some upper garments—a coat and waistcoat, Mr. Ledbetter inferred—and casting them over the rail of the bed remained breathing less noisily, and as it seemed cooling from a considerable temperature. At intervals he muttered to himself, and once he laughed softly. And Mr. Ledbetter muttered to himself, but he did not laugh. "Of all the foolish things," said Mr. Ledbetter. "What on earth am I to do now?"

His outlook was necessarily limited. The minute apertures between the stitches of the fabric of the valance admitted a certain amount of light, but permitted no peeping. The shadows upon this curtain, save for those sharply defined legs, were enigmatical, and intermingled confusingly with the florid patterning of the chintz. Beneath the edge of the valance a strip of carpet was visible, and, by cautiously depressing his eye, Mr. Ledbetter found that this strip broadened until the whole area of the floor came into view. The carpet was a luxurious one, the room spacious, and, to judge by the castors and so forth of the furniture, well equipped.

What he should do he found it difficult to imagine. To wait until this person had gone to bed, and then, when he seemed to be sleeping, to creep to the door, unlock it, and bolt headlong for that balcony seemed the only possible thing to do. Would it be possible to jump from the balcony? The danger of it! When he thought of the chances against him, Mr. Ledbetter despaired. He was within an ace of thrusting forth his head beside the gentleman's legs, coughing if necessary to attract his attention, and then, smiling, apologising and explaining his unfortunate intrusion by a few well-chosen sentences. But he found these sentences hard to choose. "No doubt, sir, my appearance is peculiar," or, "I trust, sir, you will pardon my somewhat ambiguous appearance from beneath you," was about as much as he could get.

Grave possibilities forced themselves on his attention. Suppose they did not believe him, what would they do to him? Would his unblemished high character count for nothing? Technically he was a burglar, beyond dispute. Following out this train of thought, he was composing a lucid apology for "this technical crime I have committed," to be delivered before sentence in the dock, when the stout gentleman got up and began walking about the room. He locked and unlocked drawers, and Mr. Ledbetter had a transient hope that he might be undressing. But, no! He seated himself at the writing-table, and began to write and then tear up documents. Presently the smell of burning cream-laid paper mingled with the odour of cigars in Mr. Ledbetter's nostrils.

"The position I had assumed," said Mr. Ledbetter when he told me of these things, "was in many respects an ill-advised one. A transverse bar beneath the bed depressed my head unduly, and threw a disproportionate share of my weight upon my hands. After a time, I experienced what is called, I believe, a crick in the neck. The pressure of my hands on the coarsely-stitched carpet speedily became painful. My knees, too, were painful, my trousers being drawn tightly over them. At that time I wore rather higher collars than I do now—two and a half inches, in fact—and I discovered what I had not remarked before, that the edge of the one I wore was frayed slightly under the chin. But much worse than these things was an itching of my face, which I could only relieve by violent grimacing—I tried to raise my hand, but the rustle of the sleeve alarmed me. After a time I had to desist from this relief also, because—happily in time—I discovered that my facial contortions were shifting my glasses down my nose. Their fall would, of course, have exposed me, and as it was they came to rest in an oblique position of by no means stable equilibrium. In addition I had a slight cold, and an intermittent desire to sneeze or sniff caused me inconvenience. In fact, quite apart from the extreme anxiety of my position, my physical discomfort became in a short time very considerable indeed. But I had to stay there motionless, nevertheless."

After an interminable time, there began a chinking sound. This deepened into a rhythm: chink, chink, chink—twenty-five chinks—a rap on the writing-table, and a grunt from the owner of the stout legs. It dawned upon Mr. Ledbetter that this chinking was the chinking of gold. He became incredulously curious as it went on. His curiosity grew. Already, if that was the case, this extraordinary man must have counted some hundreds of pounds. At last Mr. Ledbetter could resist it no longer, and he began very cautiously to fold his arms and lower his head to the level of the floor, in the hope of peeping under the valance. He moved his feet, and one made a slight scraping on the floor. Suddenly the chinking ceased. Mr. Ledbetter became rigid. After a while the chinking was resumed. Then it ceased again, and everything was still, except Mr. Ledbetter's heart—that organ seemed to him to be beating like a drum.

The stillness continued. Mr. Ledbetter's head was now on the floor, and he could see the stout legs as far as the shins. They were quite still. The feet were resting on the toes and drawn back, as it seemed, under the chair of the owner. Everything was quite still, everything continued still. A wild hope came to Mr. Ledbetter that the unknown was in a fit or suddenly dead, with his head upon the writing-table....

The stillness continued. What had happened? The desire to peep became irresistible. Very cautiously Mr. Ledbetter shifted his hand forward, projected a pioneer finger, and began to lift the valance immediately next his eye. Nothing broke the stillness. He saw now the stranger's knees, saw the back of the writing-table, and then—he was staring at the barrel of a heavy revolver pointed over the writing-table at his head.

"Come out of that, you scoundrel!" said the voice of the stout gentleman in a tone of quiet concentration. "Come out. This side, and now. None of your hanky-panky—come right out, now."

Mr. Ledbetter came right out, a little reluctantly perhaps, but without any hanky-panky, and at once, even as he was told.

"Kneel," said the stout gentleman, "and hold up your hands."

The valance dropped again behind Mr. Ledbetter, and he rose from all-fours and held up his hands. "Dressed like a parson," said the stout gentleman. "I'm blest if he isn't! A little chap, too! You SCOUNDREL! What the deuce possessed you to come here to-night? What the deuce possessed you to get under my bed?"

He did not appear to require an answer, but proceeded at once to several very objectionable remarks upon Mr. Ledbetter's personal appearance. He was not a very big man, but he looked strong to Mr. Ledbetter: he was as stout as his legs had promised, he had rather delicately-chiselled small features distributed over a considerable area of whitish face, and quite a number of chins. And the note of his voice had a sort of whispering undertone.

"What the deuce, I say, possessed you to get under my bed?"

Mr. Ledbetter, by an effort, smiled a wan propitiatory smile. He coughed. "I can quite understand—" he said.

"Why! What on earth? It's SOAP! No!—you scoundrel. Don't you move that hand."

"It's soap," said Mr. Ledbetter. "From your washstand. No doubt it—"

"Don't talk," said the stout man. "I see it's soap. Of all incredible things."

"If I might explain—"

"Don't explain. It's sure to be a lie, and there's no time for explanations. What was I going to ask you? Ah! Have you any mates?"

"In a few minutes, if you—"

"Have you any mates? Curse you. If you start any soapy palaver I'll shoot. Have you any mates?"

"No," said Mr. Ledbetter.

"I suppose it's a lie," said the stout man. "But you'll pay for it if it is. Why the deuce didn't you floor me when I came upstairs? You won't get a chance to now, anyhow. Fancy getting under the bed! I reckon it's a fair cop, anyhow, so far as you are concerned."

"I don't see how I could prove an alibi," remarked Mr. Ledbetter, trying to show by his conversation that he was an educated man. There was a pause. Mr. Ledbetter perceived that on a chair beside his captor was a large black bag on a heap of crumpled papers, and that there were torn and burnt papers on the table. And in front of these, and arranged methodically along the edge were rows and rows of little yellow rouleaux—a hundred times more gold than Mr. Ledbetter had seen in all his life before. The light of two candles, in silver candlesticks, fell upon these. The pause continued. "It is rather fatiguing holding up my hands like this," said Mr. Ledbetter, with a deprecatory smile.

"That's all right," said the fat man. "But what to do with you I don't exactly know."

"I know my position is ambiguous."

"Lord!" said the fat man, "ambiguous! And goes about with his own soap, and wears a thundering great clerical collar. You ARE a blooming burglar, you are—if ever there was one!"

"To be strictly accurate," said Mr. Ledbetter, and suddenly his glasses slipped off and clattered against his vest buttons.

The fat man changed countenance, a flash of savage resolution crossed his face, and something in the revolver clicked. He put his other hand to the weapon. And then he looked at Mr. Ledbetter, and his eye went down to the dropped pince-nez.

"Full-cock now, anyhow," said the fat man, after a pause, and his breath seemed to catch. "But I'll tell you, you've never been so near death before.

Lord! I'M almost glad. If it hadn't been that the revolver wasn't cocked you'd be lying dead there now."

Mr. Ledbetter said nothing, but he felt that the room was swaying.

"A miss is as good as a mile. It's lucky for both of us it wasn't. Lord!" He blew noisily. "There's no need for you to go pale-green for a little thing like that."

"If I can assure you, sir—" said Mr. Ledbetter, with an effort.

"There's only one thing to do. If I call in the police, I'm bust—a little game I've got on is bust. That won't do. If I tie you up and leave you again, the thing may be out to-morrow. Tomorrow's Sunday, and Monday's Bank Holiday—I've counted on three clear days. Shooting you's murder—and hanging; and besides, it will bust the whole blooming kernooze. I'm hanged if I can think what to do—I'm hanged if I can."

"Will you permit me—"

"You gas as much as if you were a real parson, I'm blessed if you don't. Of all the burglars you are the—Well! No!—I WON'T permit you. There isn't time. If you start off jawing again, I'll shoot right in your stomach. See? But I know now-I know now! What we're going to do first, my man, is an examination for concealed arms—an examination for concealed arms. And look here! When I tell you to do a thing, don't start off at a gabble—do it brisk."

And with many elaborate precautions, and always pointing the pistol at Mr. Ledbetter's head, the stout man stood him up and searched him for weapons. "Why, you ARE a burglar!" he said "You're a perfect amateur. You haven't even a pistol-pocket in the back of your breeches. No, you don't! Shut up, now."

So soon as the issue was decided, the stout man made Mr. Ledbetter take off his coat and roll up his shirt-sleeves, and, with the revolver at one ear, proceed with the packing his appearance had interrupted. From the stout man's point of view that was evidently the only possible arrangement, for if he had packed, he would have had to put down the revolver. So that even the gold on the table was handled by Mr. Ledbetter. This nocturnal packing was peculiar. The stout man's idea was evidently to distribute the weight of the gold as unostentatiously as possible through his luggage. It was by no means an inconsiderable weight. There was, Mr. Ledbetter says, altogether nearly L18,000 in gold in the black bag and on the table. There were also many little rolls of L5 bank-notes. Each rouleau of L25 was wrapped by Mr. Ledbetter in paper. These rouleaux were then put neatly in cigar boxes and distributed between a travelling trunk, a Gladstone bag, and a hatbox. About

L600 went in a tobacco tin in a dressing-bag. L10 in gold and a number of L5 notes the stout man pocketed. Occasionally he objurgated Mr. Ledbetter's clumsiness, and urged him to hurry, and several times he appealed to Mr. Ledbetter's watch for information.

Mr. Ledbetter strapped the trunk and bag, and returned the stout man the keys. It was then ten minutes to twelve, and until the stroke of midnight the stout man made him sit on the Gladstone bag, while he sat at a reasonably safe distance on the trunk and held the revolver handy and waited. He appeared to be now in a less aggressive mood, and having watched Mr. Ledbetter for some time, he offered a few remarks.

"From your accent I judge you are a man of some education," he said, lighting a cigar. "No—DON'T begin that explanation of yours. I know it will be long-winded from your face, and I am much too old a liar to be interested in other men's lying. You are, I say, a person of education. You do well to dress as a curate. Even among educated people you might pass as a curate."

"I AM a curate," said Mr. Ledbetter, "or, at least—"

"You are trying to be. I know. But you didn't ought to burgle. You are not the man to burgle. You are, if I may say it—the thing will have been pointed out to you before—a coward."

"Do you know," said Mr. Ledbetter, trying to get a final opening, "it was that very question—"

The stout man waved him into silence.

"You waste your education in burglary. You should do one of two things. Either you should forge or you should embezzle. For my own part, I embezzle. Yes; I embezzle. What do you think a man could be doing with all this gold but that? Ah! Listen! Midnight!... Ten. Eleven. Twelve. There is something very impressive to me in that slow beating of the hours. Time—space; what mysteries they are! What mysteries.... It's time for us to be moving. Stand up!"

And then kindly, but firmly, he induced Mr. Ledbetter to sling the dressing bag over his back by a string across his chest, to shoulder the trunk, and, overruling a gasping protest, to take the Gladstone bag in his disengaged hand. So encumbered, Mr. Ledbetter struggled perilously downstairs. The stout gentleman followed with an overcoat, the hatbox, and the revolver, making derogatory remarks about Mr. Ledbetter's strength, and assisting him at the turnings of the stairs.

"The back door," he directed, and Mr. Ledbetter staggered through a conservatory, leaving a wake of smashed flower-pots behind him. "Never mind the crockery," said the stout man; "it's good for trade. We wait here until a quarter past. You can put those things down. You have!"

Mr. Ledbetter collapsed panting on the trunk. "Last night," he gasped, "I was asleep in my little room, and I no more dreamt—"

"There's no need for you to incriminate yourself," said the stout gentleman, looking at the lock of the revolver. He began to hum. Mr. Ledbetter made to speak, and thought better of it.

There presently came the sound of a bell, and Mr. Ledbetter was taken to the back door and instructed to open it. A fair-haired man in yachting costume entered. At the sight of Mr. Ledbetter he started violently and clapped his hand behind him. Then he saw the stout man. "Bingham!" he cried, "who's this?"

"Only a little philanthropic do of mine—burglar I'm trying to reform. Caught him under my bed just now. He's all right. He's a frightful ass. He'll be useful to carry some of our things."

The newcomer seemed inclined to resent Mr. Ledbetter's presence at first, but the stout man reassured him.

"He's quite alone. There's not a gang in the world would own him. No!—don't start talking, for goodness' sake."

They went out into the darkness of the garden with the trunk still bowing Mr. Ledbetter's shoulders. The man in the yachting costume walked in front with the Gladstone bag and a pistol; then came Mr. Ledbetter like Atlas; Mr. Bingham followed with the hat-box, coat, and revolver as before. The house was one of those that have their gardens right up to the cliff. At the cliff was a steep wooden stairway, descending to a bathing tent dimly visible on the beach. Below was a boat pulled up, and a silent little man with a black face stood beside it. "A few moments' explanation," said Mr. Ledbetter; "I can assure you—" Somebody kicked him, and he said no more.

They made him wade to the boat, carrying the trunk, they pulled him aboard by the shoulders and hair, they called him no better name than "scoundrel" and "burglar" all that night. But they spoke in undertones so that the general public was happily unaware of his ignominy. They hauled him aboard a yacht manned by strange, unsympathetic Orientals, and partly they thrust him and partly he fell down a gangway into a noisome, dark place, where he was to remain many days—how many he does not know, because he lost count among other things when he was seasick. They fed him on biscuits and incomprehensible words; they gave him water to drink mixed with unwished-for rum. And there were cockroaches where they put him, night and day there were cockroaches, and in the night-time there were rats. The Orientals emptied his pockets and took his watch—but Mr. Bingham, being appealed to, took that himself. And five or six times the five Lascars—if they were Lascars—and the Chinaman and the negro who constituted the crew, fished him out and took him aft to Bingham and his friend to play cribbage and euchre and three-anded whist, and to listen to their stories and boastings in an interested manner.

Then these principals would talk to him as men talk to those who have lived a life of crime. Explanations they would never permit, though they made it abundantly clear to him that he was the rummiest burglar they had ever set eyes on. They said as much again and again. The fair man was of a taciturn disposition and irascible at play; but Mr. Bingham, now that the evident anxiety of his departure from England was assuaged, displayed a vein of genial philosophy. He enlarged upon the mystery of space and time, and quoted Kant and Hegel—or, at least, he said he did. Several times Mr. Ledbetter got as far as: "My position under your bed, you know—," but then he always had to cut, or pass the whisky, or do some such intervening thing. After his third failure, the fair man got quite to look for this opening, and whenever Mr. Ledbetter began after that, he would roar with laughter and hit him violently on the back. "Same old start, same old story; good old burglar!" the fair-haired man would say.

So Mr. Ledbetter suffered for many days, twenty perhaps; and one evening he was taken, together with some tinned provisions, over the side and put ashore on a rocky little island with a spring. Mr. Bingham came in the boat with him, giving him good advice all the way, and waving his last attempts at an explanation aside.

"I am really NOT a burglar," said Mr. Ledbetter.

"You never will be," said Mr. Bingham. "You'll never make a burglar. I'm glad you are beginning to see it. In choosing a profession a man must study his temperament. If you don't, sooner or later you will fail. Compare myself, for example. All my life I have been in banks—I have got on in banks. I have even been a bank manager. But was I happy? No. Why wasn't I happy? Because it did not suit my temperament. I am too adventurous—too versatile. Practically I have thrown it over. I do not suppose I shall ever manage a bank again. They would be glad to get me, no doubt; but I have learnt the lesson of my temperament—at last…. No! I shall never manage a bank again.

"Now, your temperament unfits you for crime—just as mine unfits me for respectability. I know you better than I did, and now I do not even recommend forgery. Go back to respectable courses, my man. YOUR lay is the philanthropic lay—that is your lay. With that voice—the Association for the Promotion of Snivelling among the Young—something in that line. You think it over.

"The island we are approaching has no name apparently—at least, there is none on the chart. You might think out a name for it while you are there—while you are thinking about all these things. It has quite drinkable water, I understand. It is one of the Grenadines—one of the Windward Islands. Yonder, dim and blue, are others of the Grenadines. There are quantities of Grenadines, but the majority are out of sight. I have often wondered what these islands are for—now, you see, I am wiser. This one at least is for you. Sooner or later some simple native will come along and take you off. Say what you like about us then—abuse us, if you like—we shan't care a solitary Grenadine! And here—here is half a sovereign's worth of silver. Do not waste that in foolish dissipation when you return to civilisation. Properly used, it may give you a fresh start in life. And do not—Don't beach her, you beggars, he can wade!—Do not waste the precious solitude before you in foolish thoughts. Properly used, it may be a turning-point in your career. Waste neither money nor time. You will die rich. I'm sorry, but I must ask you to carry your tucker to land in your arms. No; it's not deep. Curse that explanation of yours! There's not time. No, no, no! I won't listen. Overboard you go!"

And the falling night found Mr. Ledbetter—the Mr. Ledbetter who had complained that adventure was dead—sitting beside his cans of food, his chin resting upon his drawn-up knees, staring through his glasses in dismal mildness over the shining, vacant sea.

He was picked up in the course of three days by a negro fisherman and taken to St. Vincent's, and from St. Vincent's he got, by the expenditure of his last coins, to Kingston, in Jamaica. And there he might have foundered. Even nowadays he is not a man of affairs, and then he was a singularly helpless person. He had not the remotest idea what he ought to do. The only thing he seems to have done was to visit all the ministers of religion he could find in the place to borrow a passage home. But he was much too dirty and incoherent—and his story far too incredible for them. I met him quite by chance. It was close upon sunset, and I was walking out after my siesta on the road to Dunn's Battery, when I met him—I was rather bored, and with a whole evening on my hands—luckily for him. He was trudging dismally towards the town. His woebegone face and the quasi-clerical cut of his dust-stained, filthy costume caught my humour. Our eyes met. He hesitated. "Sir," he said, with a catching of the breath, "could you spare a few minutes for what I fear will seem an incredible story?"

"Incredible!" I said.

"Quite," he answered eagerly. "No one will believe it, alter it though I may. Yet I can assure you, sir—"

He stopped hopelessly. The man's tone tickled me. He seemed an odd character. "I am," he said, "one of the most unfortunate beings alive."

"Among other things, you haven't dined?" I said, struck with an idea.

"I have not," he said solemnly, "for many days."

"You'll tell it better after that," I said; and without more ado led the way to a low place I knew, where such a costume as his was unlikely to give offence. And there—with certain omissions which he subsequently supplied—I got his story. At first I was incredulous, but as the wine warmed him, and the faint suggestion of cringing which his misfortunes had added to his manner disappeared, I began to believe. At last, I was so far convinced of his sincerity that I got him a bed for the night, and next day verified the banker's reference he gave me through my Jamaica banker. And that done, I took him shopping for underwear and such like equipments of a gentleman at large. Presently came the verified reference. His astonishing story was true. I will not amplify our subsequent proceedings. He started for England in three days' time.

"I do not know how I can possibly thank you enough," began the letter he wrote me from England, "for all your kindness to a total stranger," and proceeded for some time in a similar strain. "Had it not been for your generous assistance, I could certainly never have returned in time for the resumption of my scholastic duties, and my few minutes of reckless folly would, perhaps, have proved my ruin. As it is, I am entangled in a tissue of lies and evasions, of the most complicated sort, to account for my sunburnt appearance and my whereabouts. I have rather carelessly told two or three different stories, not realising the trouble this would mean for me in the end. The truth I dare not tell. I have consulted a number of law-books in the British Museum, and there is not the slightest doubt that I have connived at and abetted and aided a felony. That scoundrel Bingham was the Hithergate bank manager, I find, and guilty of the most flagrant embezzlement. Please, please burn this letter when read—I trust you implicitly. The worst of it is, neither my aunt nor her friend who kept the boarding-house at which I was staying seem altogether to believe a guarded statement I have made them practically of what actually happened. They suspect me of some discreditable adventure, but what sort of discreditable adventure they suspect me of, I do not know. My aunt says she would forgive me if I told her everything. I have—I have told her MORE than everything, and still she is not satisfied. It would never do to let them know the truth of the case, of course, and so I represent myself as having been waylaid and gagged upon the beach. My aunt wants to know WHY they waylaid and gagged me, why they took me away in their yacht. I do not know. Can you suggest any reason? I can think of nothing. If, when you wrote, you could write on TWO sheets so that I could show her one, and on that one if you could show clearly that I really WAS in Jamaica this summer, and had come there by being removed from a ship, it would be of great service to me. It would certainly add to the load of my obligation to you—a load that I fear I can never fully repay. Although if gratitude..." And so forth. At the end he repeated his request for me to burn the letter.

So the remarkable story of Mr. Ledbetter's Vacation ends. That breach with his aunt was not of long duration. The old lady had forgiven him before she died.

10. THE STOLEN BODY

Mr. Bessel was the senior partner in the firm of Bessel, Hart, and Brown, of St. Paul's Churchyard, and for many years he was well known among those interested in psychical research as a liberal-minded and conscientious investigator. He was an unmarried man, and instead of living in the suburbs, after the fashion of his class, he occupied rooms in the Albany, near Piccadilly. He was particularly interested in the questions of thought transference and of apparitions of the living, and in November, 1896, he commenced a series of experiments in conjunction with Mr. Vincey, of Staple Inn, in order to test the alleged possibility of projecting an apparition of one's self by force of will through space.

Their experiments were conducted in the following manner: At a pre-arranged hour Mr. Bessel shut himself in one of his rooms in the Albany and Mr. Vincey in his sitting-room in Staple Inn, and each then fixed his mind as resolutely as possible on the other. Mr. Bessel had acquired the art of self-hypnotism, and, so far as he could, he attempted first to hypnotise himself and then to project himself as a "phantom of the living" across the intervening space of nearly two miles into Mr. Vincey's apartment. On several evenings this was tried without any satisfactory result, but on the fifth or sixth occasion Mr. Vincey did actually see or imagine he saw an apparition of Mr. Bessel standing in his room. He states that the appearance, although brief, was very vivid and real. He noticed that Mr. Bessel's face was white and his expression anxious, and, moreover, that his hair was disordered. For a moment Mr. Vincey, in spite of his state of expectation, was too surprised to speak or move, and in that moment it seemed to him as though the figure glanced over its shoulder and incontinently vanished.

It had been arranged that an attempt should be made to photograph any phantasm seen, but Mr. Vincey had not the instant presence of mind to snap the camera that lay ready on the table beside him, and when he did so he was too late. Greatly elated, however, even by this partial success, he made a note of the exact time, and at once took a cab to the Albany to inform Mr. Bessel of this result.

He was surprised to find Mr. Bessel's outer door standing open to the night, and the inner apartments lit and in an extraordinary disorder. An empty champagne magnum lay smashed upon the floor; its neck had been broken off against the inkpot on the bureau and lay beside it. An octagonal occasional table, which carried a bronze statuette and a number of choice books, had been rudely overturned, and down the primrose paper of the wall inky fingers had been drawn, as it seemed for the mere pleasure of defilement. One of the delicate chintz curtains had been violently torn from its rings and thrust upon the fire, so that the smell of its smouldering filled the room. Indeed the whole place was disarranged in the strangest fashion. For a few minutes Mr. Vincey, who had entered sure of finding Mr. Bessel in his easy chair awaiting him, could scarcely believe his eyes, and stood staring helplessly at these unanticipated things.

Then, full of a vague sense of calamity, he sought the porter at the entrance lodge. "Where is Mr. Bessel?" he asked. "Do you know that all the furniture is broken in Mr. Bessel's room?" The porter said nothing, but, obeying his gestures, came at once to Mr. Bessel's apartment to see the state of affairs. "This settles it," he said, surveying the lunatic confusion. "I didn't know of this. Mr. Bessel's gone off. He's mad!"

He then proceeded to tell Mr. Vincey that about half an hour previously, that is to say, at about the time of Mr. Bessel's apparition in Mr. Vincey's rooms, the missing gentleman had rushed out of the gates of the Albany into Vigo Street, hatless and with disordered hair, and had vanished into the direction of Bond Street. "And as he went past me," said the porter, "he laughed—a sort of gasping laugh, with his mouth open and his eyes glaring—I tell you, sir, he fair scared me!—like this."

According to his imitation it was anything but a pleasant laugh. "He waved his hand, with all his fingers crooked and clawing—like that. And he said, in a sort of fierce whisper, 'LIFE!' Just that one word, 'LIFE!'"

"Dear me," said Mr. Vincey. "Tut, tut," and "Dear me!" He could think of nothing else to say. He was naturally very much surprised. He turned from the room to the porter and from the porter to the room in the gravest perplexity. Beyond his suggestion that probably Mr. Bessel would come back presently and explain what had happened, their conversation was unable to proceed. "It might be a sudden toothache," said the porter, "a very sudden and violent toothache, jumping on him suddenly-like and driving him wild. I've broken things myself before now in such a case..." He thought. "If it was, why should he say 'LIFE' to me as he went past?"

Mr. Vincey did not know. Mr. Bessel did not return, and at last Mr. Vincey, having done some more helpless staring, and having addressed a note of brief inquiry and left it in a conspicuous position on the bureau, returned in a very perplexed frame of mind to his own premises in Staple Inn. This affair had given him a shock. He was at a loss to account for Mr. Bessel's conduct on any sane hypothesis. He tried to read, but he could not do so; he went for a short walk, and was so preoccupied that he narrowly escaped a cab at the top of Chancery Lane; and at last—a full hour before his usual time—he went to bed. For a considerable time he could not sleep because of his memory of the silent confusion of Mr. Bessel's apartment, and when at length he did attain an uneasy slumber it was at once disturbed by a very vivid and distressing dream of Mr. Bessel.

He saw Mr. Bessel gesticulating wildly, and with his face white and contorted. And, inexplicably mingled with his appearance, suggested perhaps by his gestures, was an intense fear, an urgency to act. He even believes that he heard the voice of his fellow experimenter calling distressfully to him, though at the time he considered this to be an illusion. The vivid impression remained though Mr. Vincey awoke. For a space he lay awake and trembling in the darkness, possessed with that vague, unaccountable terror of unknown possibilities that comes out of dreams upon even the bravest men. But at last he roused himself, and turned over and went to sleep again, only for the dream to return with enhanced vividness.

He awoke with such a strong conviction that Mr. Bessel was in overwhelming distress and need of help that sleep was no longer possible. He was persuaded that his friend had rushed out to some dire calamity. For a time he lay reasoning vainly against this belief, but at last he gave way to it. He arose, against all reason, lit his gas, and dressed, and set out through the deserted streets—deserted, save for a noiseless policeman or so and the early news carts—towards Vigo Street to inquire if Mr. Bessel had returned.

But he never got there. As he was going down Long Acre some unaccountable impulse turned him aside out of that street towards Covent Garden, which was just waking to its nocturnal activities. He saw the market in front of him—a queer effect of glowing yellow lights and busy black figures. He became aware of a shouting, and perceived a figure turn the corner by the hotel and run swiftly towards him. He knew at once that it was Mr. Bessel. But it was Mr. Bessel transfigured. He was hatless and dishevelled, his collar was torn open, he grasped a bone-handled walking-cane near the ferrule end, and his mouth was pulled awry. And he ran, with agile strides, very rapidly. Their encounter was the affair of an instant. "Bessel!" cried Vincey.

The running man gave no sign of recognition either of Mr. Vincey or of his own name. Instead, he cut at his friend savagely with the stick, hitting him in the face within an inch of the eye. Mr. Vincey, stunned and astonished, staggered back, lost his footing, and fell heavily on the pavement. It seemed to him that Mr. Bessel leapt over him as he fell. When he looked again Mr. Bessel had vanished, and a policeman and a number of garden porters and salesmen were rushing past towards Long Acre in hot pursuit.

With the assistance of several passers-by—for the whole street was speedily alive with running people—Mr. Vincey struggled to his feet. He at once became the centre of a crowd greedy to see his injury. A multitude of voices competed to reassure him of his safety, and then to tell him of the behaviour of the madman, as they regarded Mr. Bessel. He had suddenly appeared in the middle of the market screaming "LIFE! LIFE!" striking left and right with a blood-stained walking-stick, and dancing and shouting with laughter at each successful blow. A lad and two women had broken heads, and he had smashed a man's wrist; a little child had been knocked insensible, and for a time he had driven every one before him, so furious and resolute had his behaviour been. Then he made a raid upon a coffee stall, hurled its paraffin flare through the window of the post office, and fled laughing, after stunning the foremost of the two policemen who had the pluck to charge him.

Mr. Vincey's first impulse was naturally to join in the pursuit of his friend, in order if possible to save him from the violence of the indignant people. But his action was slow, the blow had half stunned him, and while this was still no more than a resolution came the news, shouted through the crowd, that Mr. Bessel had eluded his pursuers. At first Mr. Vincey could scarcely credit this, but the universality of the report, and presently the dignified return of two futile policemen, convinced him. After some aimless inquiries he returned towards Staple Inn, padding a handkerchief to a now very painful nose.

He was angry and astonished and perplexed. It appeared to him indisputable that Mr. Bessel must have gone violently mad in the midst of his experiment in thought transference, but why that should make him appear with a sad white face in Mr. Vincey's dreams seemed a problem beyond solution. He racked his brains in vain to explain this. It seemed to him at last that not simply Mr. Bessel, but the order of things must be insane. But he could think of nothing to do. He shut himself carefully into his room, lit his fire—it was a gas fire with asbestos bricks—and, fearing fresh dreams if he went to bed, remained bathing his injured face, or holding up books in a vain attempt to read, until dawn. Throughout that vigil he had a curious persuasion that Mr. Bessel was endeavouring to speak to him, but he would not let himself attend to any such belief.

About dawn, his physical fatigue asserted itself, and he went to bed and slept at last in spite of dreaming. He rose late, unrested and anxious, and in considerable facial pain. The morning papers had no news of Mr. Bessel's aberration—it had come too late for them. Mr. Vincey's perplexities, to which the fever of his bruise added fresh irritation, became at last intolerable, and, after a fruitless visit to the Albany, he went down to St. Paul's Churchyard to Mr. Hart, Mr. Bessel's partner, and, so far as Mr. Vincey knew, his nearest friend.

He was surprised to learn that Mr. Hart, although he knew nothing of the outbreak, had also been disturbed by a vision, the very vision that Mr. Vincey had seen—Mr. Bessel, white and dishevelled, pleading earnestly by his gestures for help. That was his impression of the import of his signs. "I was just going to look him up in the Albany when you arrived," said Mr. Hart. "I was so sure of something being wrong with him."

As the outcome of their consultation the two gentlemen decided to inquire at Scotland Yard for news of their missing friend. "He is bound to be laid by the heels," said Mr. Hart. "He can't go on at that pace for long." But the police authorities had not laid Mr. Bessel by the heels. They confirmed Mr. Vincey's overnight experiences and added fresh circumstances, some of an even graver character than those he knew—a list of smashed glass along the upper half of Tottenham Court Road, an attack upon a policeman in Hampstead Road, and an atrocious assault upon a woman. All these outrages were committed between half-past twelve and a quarter to two in the morning, and between those hours—and, indeed, from the very moment of Mr. Bessel's first rush from his rooms at half-past nine in the evening—they could trace the deepening violence of his fantastic career. For the last hour, at least from before one, that is, until a quarter to two, he had run amuck through London, eluding with amazing agility every effort to stop or capture him.

But after a quarter to two he had vanished. Up to that hour witnesses were multitudinous. Dozens of people had seen him, fled from him or pursued him, and then things suddenly came to an end. At a quarter to two he had been seen running down the Euston Road towards Baker Street, flourishing a can of burning colza oil and jerking splashes of flame therefrom at the windows of the houses he passed. But none of the policemen on Euston Road beyond the Waxwork Exhibition, nor any of those in the side streets down which he must have passed had he left the Euston Road, had seen anything of him. Abruptly he disappeared. Nothing of his subsequent doings came to light in spite of the keenest inquiry.

Here was a fresh astonishment for Mr. Vincey. He had found considerable comfort in Mr. Hart's conviction: "He is bound to be laid by the heels before long," and in that assurance he had been able to suspend his mental perplexities. But any fresh development seemed destined to add new impossibilities to a pile already heaped beyond the powers of his acceptance. He found himself doubting whether his memory might not have played him some grotesque trick, debating whether any of these things could possibly have happened; and in the afternoon he hunted up Mr. Hart again to share the intolerable weight on his mind. He found Mr. Hart engaged with a well-known private detective, but as that gentleman accomplished nothing in this case, we need not enlarge upon his proceedings.

All that day Mr. Bessel's whereabouts eluded an unceasingly active inquiry, and all that night. And all that day there was a persuasion in the back of

Vincey's mind that Mr. Bessel sought his attention, and all through the night Mr. Bessel with a tear-stained face of anguish pursued him through his dreams. And whenever he saw Mr. Bessel in his dreams he also saw a number of other faces, vague but malignant, that seemed to be pursuing Mr. Bessel.

It was on the following day, Sunday, that Mr. Vincey recalled certain remarkable stories of Mrs. Bullock, the medium, who was then attracting attention for the first time in London. He determined to consult her. She was staying at the house of that well-known inquirer, Dr. Wilson Paget, and Mr. Vincey, although he had never met that gentleman before, repaired to him forthwith with the intention of invoking her help. But scarcely had he mentioned the name of Bessel when Doctor Paget interrupted him. "Last night—just at the end," he said, "we had a communication."

He left the room, and returned with a slate on which were certain words written in a handwriting, shaky indeed, but indisputably the handwriting of Mr. Bessel!

"How did you get this?" said Mr. Vincey. "Do you mean—?"

"We got it last night," said Doctor Paget. With numerous interruptions from Mr. Vincey, he proceeded to explain how the writing had been obtained. It appears that in her seances, Mrs. Bullock passes into a condition of trance, her eyes rolling up in a strange way under her eyelids, and her body becoming rigid. She then begins to talk very rapidly, usually in voices other than her own. At the same time one or both of her hands may become active, and if slates and pencils are provided they will then write messages simultaneously with and quite independently of the flow of words from her mouth. By many she is considered an even more remarkable medium than the celebrated Mrs. Piper. It was one of these messages, the one written by her left hand, that Mr. Vincey now had before him. It consisted of eight words written disconnectedly: "George Bessel... trial excavn.... Baker Street... help... starvation." Curiously enough, neither Doctor Paget nor the two other inquirers who were present had heard of the disappearance of Mr. Bessel— the news of it appeared only in the evening papers of Saturday—and they had put the message aside with many others of a vague and enigmatical sort that Mrs. Bullock has from time to time delivered.

When Doctor Paget heard Mr. Vincey's story, he gave himself at once with great energy to the pursuit of this clue to the discovery of Mr. Bessel. It would serve no useful purpose here to describe the inquiries of Mr. Vincey and himself; suffice it that the clue was a genuine one, and that Mr. Bessel was actually discovered by its aid.

He was found at the bottom of a detached shaft which had been sunk and abandoned at the commencement of the work for the new electric railway near Baker Street Station. His arm and leg and two ribs were broken. The shaft is protected by a hoarding nearly 20 feet high, and over this, incredible as it seems, Mr. Bessel, a stout, middle-aged gentleman, must have scrambled in order to fall down the shaft. He was saturated in colza oil, and the smashed tin lay beside him, but luckily the flame had been extinguished by his fall. And his madness had passed from him altogether. But he was, of course, terribly enfeebled, and at the sight of his rescuers he gave way to hysterical weeping.

In view of the deplorable state of his flat, he was taken to the house of Dr. Hatton in Upper Baker Street. Here he was subjected to a sedative treatment, and anything that might recall the violent crisis through which he had passed was carefully avoided. But on the second day he volunteered a statement.

Since that occasion Mr. Bessel has several times repeated this statement—to myself among other people—varying the details as the narrator of real experiences always does, but never by any chance contradicting himself in any particular. And the statement he makes is in substance as follows.

In order to understand it clearly it is necessary to go back to his experiments with Mr. Vincey before his remarkable attack. Mr. Bessel's first attempts at self-projection, in his experiments with Mr. Vincey, were, as the reader will remember, unsuccessful. But through all of them he was concentrating all his power and will upon getting out of the body—"willing it with all my might," he says. At last, almost against expectation, came success. And Mr. Bessel asserts that he, being alive, did actually, by an effort of will, leave his body and pass into some place or state outside this world.

The release was, he asserts, instantaneous. "At one moment I was seated in my chair, with my eyes tightly shut, my hands gripping the arms of the chair, doing all I could to concentrate my mind on Vincey, and then I perceived myself outside my body—saw my body near me, but certainly not containing me, with the hands relaxing and the head drooping forward on the breast."

Nothing shakes him in his assurance of that release. He describes in a quiet, matter-of-fact way the new sensation he experienced. He felt he had become impalpable—so much he had expected, but he had not expected to find himself enormously large. So, however, it would seem he became. "I was a great cloud—if I may express it that way—anchored to my body. It appeared to me, at first, as if I had discovered a greater self of which the conscious being in my brain was only a little part. I saw the Albany and Piccadilly and Regent Street and all the rooms and places in the houses, very minute and very bright and distinct, spread out below me like a little city seen from a balloon. Every now and then vague shapes like drifting wreaths of smoke made the vision a little indistinct, but at first I paid little heed to them. The thing that astonished me most, and which astonishes me still, is that I saw quite distinctly the insides of the houses as well as the streets, saw little people dining and talking in the private houses, men and women dining, playing billiards, and drinking in restaurants and hotels, and several places of entertainment crammed with people. It was like watching the affairs of a glass hive."

Such were Mr. Bessel's exact words as I took them down when he told me the story. Quite forgetful of Mr. Vincey, he remained for a space observing these things. Impelled by curiosity, he says, he stooped down, and, with the shadowy arm he found himself possessed of, attempted to touch a man walking along Vigo Street. But he could not do so, though his finger seemed to pass through the man. Something prevented his doing this, but what it was he finds it hard to describe. He compares the obstacle to a sheet of glass.

"I felt as a kitten may feel," he said, "when it goes for the first time to pat its reflection in a mirror." Again and again, on the occasion when I heard him tell this story, Mr. Bessel returned to that comparison of the sheet of glass. Yet it was not altogether a precise comparison, because, as the reader will speedily see, there were interruptions of this generally impermeable resistance, means of getting through the barrier to the material world again. But, naturally, there is a very great difficulty in expressing these unprecedented impressions in the language of everyday experience.

A thing that impressed him instantly, and which weighed upon him throughout all this experience, was the stillness of this place—he was in a world without sound.

At first Mr. Bessel's mental state was an unemotional wonder. His thought chiefly concerned itself with where he might be. He was out of the body—out of his material body, at any rate—but that was not all. He believes, and I for one believe also, that he was somewhere out of space, as we understand it, altogether. By a strenuous effort of will he had passed out of his body into a world beyond this world, a world undreamt of, yet lying so close to it and so strangely situated with regard to it that all things on this earth are clearly visible both from without and from within in this other world about us. For a long time, as it seemed to him, this realisation occupied his mind to the exclusion of all other matters, and then he recalled the engagement with Mr. Vincey, to which this astonishing experience was, after all, but a prelude.

He turned his mind to locomotion in this new body in which he found himself. For a time he was unable to shift himself from his attachment to his earthly carcass. For a time this new strange cloud body of his simply swayed, contracted, expanded, coiled, and writhed with his efforts to free himself, and then quite suddenly the link that bound him snapped. For a moment everything was hidden by what appeared to be whirling spheres of dark vapour, and then through a momentary gap he saw his drooping body collapse limply, saw his lifeless head drop sideways, and found he was driving along like a huge cloud in a strange place of shadowy clouds that had the luminous intricacy of London spread like a model below.

But now he was aware that the fluctuating vapour about him was something more than vapour, and the temerarious excitement of his first essay was shot with fear. For he perceived, at first indistinctly, and then suddenly very clearly, that he was surrounded by FACES! that each roll and coil of the seeming cloud-stuff was a face. And such faces! Faces of thin shadow, faces of gaseous tenuity. Faces like those faces that glare with intolerable strangeness upon the sleeper in the evil hours of his dreams. Evil, greedy eyes that were full of a covetous curiosity, faces with knit brows and snarling, smiling lips; their vague hands clutched at Mr. Bessel as he passed, and the rest of their bodies was but an elusive streak of trailing darkness. Never a word they said, never a sound from the mouths that seemed to gibber. All about him they pressed in that dreamy silence, passing freely through the dim mistiness that was his body, gathering ever more numerously about him. And the shadowy Mr. Bessel, now suddenly fear-stricken, drove through the silent, active multitude of eyes and clutching hands.

So inhuman were these faces, so malignant their staring eyes, and shadowy, clawing gestures, that it did not occur to Mr. Bessel to attempt intercourse with these drifting creatures. Idiot phantoms, they seemed, children of vain desire, beings unborn and forbidden the boon of being, whose only expressions and gestures told of the envy and craving for life that was their one link with existence.

It says much for his resolution that, amidst the swarming cloud of these noiseless spirits of evil, he could still think of Mr. Vincey. He made a violent effort of will and found himself, he knew not how, stooping towards Staple Inn, saw Vincey sitting attentive and alert in his arm-chair by the fire.

And clustering also about him, as they clustered ever about all that lives and breathes, was another multitude of these vain voiceless shadows, longing, desiring, seeking some loophole into life.

For a space Mr. Bessel sought ineffectually to attract his friend's attention. He tried to get in front of his eyes, to move the objects in his room, to touch him. But Mr. Vincey remained unaffected, ignorant of the being that was so close to his own. The strange something that Mr. Bessel has compared to a sheet of glass separated them impermeably.

And at last Mr. Bessel did a desperate thing. I have told how that in some strange way he could see not only the outside of a man as we see him, but within. He extended his shadowy hand and thrust his vague black fingers, as it seemed, through the heedless brain.

Then, suddenly, Mr. Vincey started like a man who recalls his attention from wandering thoughts, and it seemed to Mr. Bessel that a little dark-red body situated in the middle of Mr. Vincey's brain swelled and glowed as he did so. Since that experience he has been shown anatomical figures of the brain, and he knows now that this is that useless structure, as doctors call it, the pineal eye. For, strange as it will seem to many, we have, deep in our brains—where it cannot possibly see any earthly light—an eye! At the time this, with the rest of the internal anatomy of the brain, was quite new to him. At the sight of its changed appearance, however, he thrust forth his finger, and, rather fearful still of the consequences, touched this little spot. And instantly Mr. Vincey started, and Mr. Bessel knew that he was seen.

And at that instant it came to Mr. Bessel that evil had happened to his body, and behold! a great wind blew through all that world of shadows and tore him away. So strong was this persuasion that he thought no more of Mr. Vincey, but turned about forthwith, and all the countless faces drove back with him like leaves before a gale. But he returned too late. In an instant he saw the body that he had left inert and collapsed—lying, indeed, like the body of a man just dead—had arisen, had arisen by virtue of some strength and will beyond his own. It stood with staring eyes, stretching its limbs in dubious fashion.

For a moment he watched it in wild dismay, and then he stooped towards it. But the pane of glass had closed against him again, and he was foiled. He beat himself passionately against this, and all about him the spirits of evil grinned and pointed and mocked. He gave way to furious anger. He compares himself to a bird that has fluttered heedlessly into a room and is beating at the window-pane that holds it back from freedom.

And behold! the little body that had once been his was now dancing with delight. He saw it shouting, though he could not hear its shouts; he saw the violence of its movements grow. He watched it fling his cherished furniture about in the mad delight of existence, rend his books apart, smash bottles, drink heedlessly from the jagged fragments, leap and smite in a passionate acceptance of living. He watched these actions in paralysed astonishment. Then once more he hurled himself against the impassable barrier, and then with all that crew of mocking ghosts about him, hurried back in dire confusion to Vincey to tell him of the outrage that had come upon him.

But the brain of Vincey was now closed against apparitions, and the disembodied Mr. Bessel pursued him in vain as he hurried out into Holborn to call a cab. Foiled and terror-stricken, Mr. Bessel swept back again, to find his desecrated body whooping in a glorious frenzy down the Burlington Arcade....

And now the attentive reader begins to understand Mr. Bessel's interpretation of the first part of this strange story. The being whose frantic rush through London had inflicted so much injury and disaster had indeed Mr. Bessel's body, but it was not Mr. Bessel. It was an evil spirit out of that strange world beyond existence, into which Mr. Bessel had so rashly ventured. For twenty hours it held possession of him, and for all those twenty hours the dispossessed spirit-body of Mr. Bessel was going to and fro in that unheard-of middle world of shadows seeking help in vain. He spent many hours beating at the minds of Mr. Vincey and of his friend Mr. Hart. Each, as we know, he roused by his efforts. But the language that might convey his situation to these helpers across the gulf he did not know; his feeble fingers groped vainly and powerlessly in their brains. Once, indeed, as we have already told, he was able to turn Mr. Vincey aside from his path so that he encountered the stolen body in its career, but he could not make him understand the thing that had happened: he was unable to draw any help from that encounter....

All through those hours the persuasion was overwhelming in Mr. Bessel's mind that presently his body would be killed by its furious tenant, and he would have to remain in this shadow-land for evermore. So that those long hours were a growing agony of fear. And ever as he hurried to and fro in his ineffectual excitement, innumerable spirits of that world about him mobbed him and confused his mind. And ever an envious applauding multitude poured after their successful fellow as he went upon his glorious career.

For that, it would seem, must be the life of these bodiless things of this world that is the shadow of our world. Ever they watch, coveting a way into a mortal body, in order that they may descend, as furies and frenzies, as violent lusts and mad, strange impulses, rejoicing in the body they have won. For Mr. Bessel was not the only human soul in that place. Witness the fact that he met first one, and afterwards several shadows of men, men like himself, it seemed, who had lost their bodies even it may be as he had lost his, and wandered, despairingly, in that lost world that is neither life nor death. They could not speak because that world is silent, yet he knew them for men because of their dim human bodies, and because of the sadness of their faces.

But how they had come into that world he could not tell, nor where the bodies they had lost might be, whether they still raved about the earth, or whether they were closed forever in death against return. That they were the spirits of the dead neither he nor I believe. But Doctor Wilson Paget thinks they are the rational souls of men who are lost in madness on the earth.

At last Mr. Bessel chanced upon a place where a little crowd of such disembodied silent creatures was gathered, and thrusting through them he saw below a brightly-lit room, and four or five quiet gentlemen and a woman, a stoutish woman dressed in black bombazine and sitting awkwardly in a chair with her head thrown back. He knew her from her portraits to be Mrs. Bullock, the medium. And he perceived that tracts and structures in her brain glowed and stirred as he had seen the pineal eye in the brain of Mr. Vincey glow. The light was very fitful; sometimes it was a broad illumination, and sometimes merely a faint twilight spot, and it shifted slowly about her brain. She kept on talking and writing with one hand. And Mr. Bessel saw that the crowding shadows of men about him, and a great multitude of the shadow spirits of that shadowland, were all striving and thrusting to touch the lighted regions of her brain. As one gained her brain or another was thrust away, her voice and the writing of her hand changed. So that what she said was disorderly and confused for the most part; now a fragment of one soul's message, and now a fragment of another's, and now she babbled the insane fancies of the spirits of vain desire. Then Mr. Bessel understood that she spoke for the spirit that had touch of her, and he began to struggle very furiously towards her. But he was on the outside of the crowd and at that time could not reach her, and at last, growing anxious, he went away to find what had happened meanwhile to his body. For a long time he went to and fro seeking it in vain and fearing that it must have been killed, and then he found it at the bottom of the shaft in Baker Street, writhing furiously and cursing with pain. Its leg and an arm and two ribs had been broken by its fall. Moreover, the evil spirit was angry because his time had been so short and because of the painmaking violent movements and casting his body about.

And at that Mr. Bessel returned with redoubled earnestness to the room where the seance was going on, and so soon as he had thrust himself within sight of the place he saw one of the men who stood about the medium looking at his watch as if he meant that the seance should presently end. At that a great number of the shadows who had been striving turned away with gestures of despair. But the thought that the seance was almost over only made Mr. Bessel the more earnest, and he struggled so stoutly with his will against the others that presently he gained the woman's brain. It chanced that just at that moment it glowed very brightly, and in that instant she wrote the message that Doctor Wilson Paget preserved. And then the other shadows and the cloud of evil spirits about him had thrust Mr. Bessel away from her, and for all the rest of the seance he could regain her no more.

So he went back and watched through the long hours at the bottom of the shaft where the evil spirit lay in the stolen body it had maimed, writhing and cursing, and weeping and groaning, and learning the lesson of pain. And towards dawn the thing he had waited for happened, the brain glowed brightly and the evil spirit came out, and Mr. Bessel entered the body he had feared he should never enter again. As he did so, the silence—the brooding silence—ended; he heard the tumult of traffic and the voices of people overhead, and that strange world that is the shadow of our world—the dark and silent shadows of ineffectual desire and the shadows of lost men—vanished clean away.

He lay there for the space of about three hours before he was found. And in spite of the pain and suffering of his wounds, and of the dim damp place in which he lay; in spite of the tears—wrung from him by his physical distress—his heart was full of gladness to know that he was nevertheless back once more in the kindly world of men.

11. MR. BRISHER'S TREASURE

"You can't be TOO careful WHO you marry," said Mr. Brisher, and pulled thoughtfully with a fat-wristed hand at the lank moustache that hides his want of chin.

"That's why—" I ventured.

"Yes," said Mr. Brisher, with a solemn light in his bleary, blue-grey eyes, moving his head expressively and breathing alcohol INTIMATELY at me. "There's lots as 'ave 'ad a try at me—many as I could name in this town—but none 'ave done it—none."

I surveyed the flushed countenance, the equatorial expansion, the masterly carelessness of his attire, and heaved a sigh to think that by reason of the unworthiness of women he must needs be the last of his race.

"I was a smart young chap when I was younger," said Mr. Brisher. "I 'ad my work cut out. But I was very careful—very. And I got through..."

He leant over the taproom table and thought visibly on the subject of my trustworthiness. I was relieved at last by his confidence.

"I was engaged once," he said at last, with a reminiscent eye on the shuv-a'penny board.

"So near as that?"

He looked at me. "So near as that. Fact is—" He looked about him, brought his face close to mine, lowered his voice, and fenced off an unsympathetic world with a grimy hand. "If she ain't dead or married to some one else or anything—I'm engaged still. Now." He confirmed this statement with nods and facial contortions. "STILL," he said, ending the pantomime, and broke into a reckless smile at my surprise. "ME!"

"Run away," he explained further, with coruscating eyebrows. "Come 'ome.

"That ain't all.

"You'd 'ardly believe it," he said, "but I found a treasure. Found a regular treasure."

I fancied this was irony, and did not, perhaps, greet it with proper surprise. "Yes," he said, "I found a treasure. And come 'ome. I tell you I could surprise you with things that has happened to me." And for some time he was content to repeat that he had found a treasure—and left it.

I made no vulgar clamour for a story, but I became attentive to Mr. Brisher's bodily needs, and presently I led him back to the deserted lady.

"She was a nice girl," he said—a little sadly, I thought. "AND respectable."

He raised his eyebrows and tightened his mouth to express extreme respectability—beyond the likes of us elderly men.

"It was a long way from 'ere. Essex, in fact. Near Colchester. It was when I was up in London—in the buildin' trade. I was a smart young chap then, I can tell you. Slim. 'Ad best clo'es 's good as anybody. 'At—SILK 'at, mind you." Mr. Brisher's hand shot above his head towards the infinite to indicate it silk hat of the highest. "Umbrella—nice umbrella with a 'orn 'andle. Savin's. Very careful I was...."

He was pensive for a little while, thinking, as we must all come to think sooner or later, of the vanished brightness of youth. But he refrained, as one may do in taprooms, from the obvious moral.

"I got to know 'er through a chap what was engaged to 'er sister. She was stopping in London for a bit with an aunt that 'ad a 'am an' beef shop. This aunt was very particular—they was all very particular people, all 'er people was—and wouldn't let 'er sister go out with this feller except 'er other sister, MY girl that is, went with them. So 'e brought me into it, sort of to ease the crowding. We used to go walks in Battersea Park of a Sunday afternoon. Me in my topper, and 'im in 'is; and the girl's—well—stylish. There wasn't many in Battersea Park 'ad the larf of us. She wasn't what you'd call pretty, but a nicer girl I never met. *I* liked 'er from the start, and, well—though I say it who shouldn't—she liked me. You know 'ow it is, I dessay?"

I pretended I did.

"And when this chap married 'er sister—'im and me was great friends—what must 'e do but arst me down to Colchester, close by where She lived. Naturally I was introjuced to 'er people, and well, very soon, her and me was engaged."

He repeated "engaged."

"She lived at 'ome with 'er father and mother, quite the lady, in a very nice little 'ouse with a garden—and remarkable respectable people they was. Rich you might call 'em a'most. They owned their own 'ouse—got it out of the Building Society, and cheap because the chap who had it before was a burglar and in prison—and they 'ad a bit of free'old land, and some cottages and money 'nvested—all nice and tight: they was what you'd call snug and warm. I tell you, I was On. Furniture too. Why! They 'ad a pianner. Jane—'er name was Jane—used to play it Sundays, and very nice she played too. There wasn't 'ardly a 'im toon in the book she COULDN'T play...

"Many's the evenin' we've met and sung 'ims there, me and 'er and the family.

"'Er father was quite a leadin' man in chapel. You should ha' seen him Sundays, interruptin' the minister and givin' out 'ims. He had gold spectacles, I remember, and used to look over 'em at you while he sang hearty—he was always great on singing 'earty to the Lord—and when HE got out o' toon 'arf the people went after 'im—always. 'E was that sort of man. And to walk be'ind 'im in 'is nice black clo'es—'is 'at was a brimmer—made one regular proud to be engaged to such a father-in-law. And when the summer came I went down there and stopped a fortnight.

"Now, you know there was a sort of Itch," said Mr. Brisher. "We wanted to marry, me and Jane did, and get things settled. But 'E said I 'ad to get a proper position first. Consequently there was a Itch. Consequently, when I went down there, I was anxious to show that I was a good useful sort of chap like. Show I could do pretty nearly everything like. See?"

I made a sympathetic noise.

"And down at the bottom of their garden was a bit of wild part like. So I says to 'im, 'Why don't you 'ave a rockery 'ere?' I says. 'It 'ud look nice.'

"'Too much expense,' he says.

"'Not a penny,' says I. 'I'm a dab at rockeries. Lemme make you one.' You see, I'd 'elped my brother make a rockery in the beer garden be'ind 'is tap, so I knew 'ow to do it to rights. 'Lemme make you one,' I says. 'It's 'olidays, but I'm that sort of chap, I 'ate doing nothing,' I says. 'I'll make you one to rights.' And the long and the short of it was, he said I might.

"And that's 'ow I come on the treasure."

"What treasure?" I asked.

"Why!" said Mr. Brisher, "the treasure I'm telling you about, what's the reason why I never married."

"What!—a treasure—dug up?"

"Yes—buried wealth—treasure trove. Come out of the ground. What I kept on saying—regular treasure...." He looked at me with unusual disrespect.

"It wasn't more than a foot deep, not the top of it," he said. "I'd 'ardly got thirsty like, before I come on the corner."

"Go on," I said. "I didn't understand."

"Why! Directly I 'it the box I knew it was treasure. A sort of instinct told me. Something seemed to shout inside of me—'Now's your chance—lie low.' It's lucky I knew the laws of treasure trove or I'd 'ave been shoutin' there and then. I daresay you know—"

"Crown bags it," I said, "all but one per cent. Go on. It's a shame. What did you do?"

"Uncovered the top of the box. There wasn't anybody in the garden or about like. Jane was 'elping 'er mother do the 'ouse. I WAS excited—I tell you. I tried the lock and then gave a whack at the hinges. Open it came. Silver coins—full! Shining. It made me tremble to see 'em. And jest then—I'm blessed if the dustman didn't come round the back of the 'ouse. It pretty nearly gave me 'eart disease to think what a fool I was to 'ave that money showing. And directly after I 'eard the chap next door—'e was 'olidaying, too—I 'eard him watering 'is beans. If only 'e'd looked over the fence!"

"What did you do?"

"Kicked the lid on again and covered it up like a shot, and went on digging about a yard away from it—like mad. And my face, so to speak, was laughing on its own account till I had it hid. I tell you I was regular scared like at my luck. I jest thought that it 'ad to be kep' close and that was all. 'Treasure,' I kep' whisperin' to myself, 'Treasure' and "undreds of pounds, 'undreds, 'undreds of pounds.' Whispering to myself like, and digging like blazes. It seemed to me the box was regular sticking out and showing, like your legs do under the sheets in bed, and I went and put all the earth I'd got out of my 'ole for the rockery slap on top of it. I WAS in a sweat. And in the midst of it all out toddles 'er father. He didn't say anything to me, jest stood behind me and stared, but Jane tole me afterwards when he went indoors, 'e says, 'That there jackanapes of yours, Jane'—he always called me a jackanapes some'ow—'knows 'ow to put 'is back into it after all.' Seemed quite impressed by it, 'e did."

"How long was the box?" I asked, suddenly.

"'Ow long?" said Mr. Brisher.

"Yes—in length?"

"Oh! 'bout so-by-so." Mr. Brisher indicated a moderate-sized trunk.

"FULL?" said I.

"Full up of silver coins—'arf-crowns, I believe."

"Why!" I cried, "that would mean—hundreds of pounds."

"Thousands," said Mr. Brisher, in a sort of sad calm. "I calc'lated it out."

"But how did they get there?"

"All I know is what I found. What I thought at the time was this. The chap who'd owned the 'ouse before 'er father 'd been a regular slap-up burglar. What you'd call a 'igh-class criminal. Used to drive 'is trap—like Peace did."

Mr. Brisher meditated on the difficulties of narration and embarked on a complicated parenthesis. "I don't know if I told you it'd been a burglar's 'ouse before it was my girl's father's, and I knew 'e'd robbed a mail train once, I did know that. It seemed to me—"

"That's very likely," I said. "But what did you do?"

"Sweated," said Mr. Brisher. "Regular run orf me. All that morning," said Mr. Brisher, "I was at it, pretending to make that rockery and wondering what I should do. I'd 'ave told 'er father p'r'aps, only I was doubtful of 'is honesty—I was afraid he might rob me of it like, and give it up to the authorities—and besides, considering I was marrying into the family, I thought it would be nicer like if it came through me. Put me on a better footing, so to speak. Well, I 'ad three days before me left of my 'olidays, so there wasn't no hurry, so I covered it up and went on digging, and tried to puzzle out 'ow I was to make sure of it. Only I couldn't.

"I thought," said Mr. Brisher, "AND I thought. Once I got regular doubtful whether I'd seen it or not, and went down to it and 'ad it uncovered again, just as her ma came out to 'ang up a bit of washin' she'd done. Jumps again! Afterwards I was just thinking I'd 'ave another go at it, when Jane comes to tell me dinner was ready. 'You'll want it,' she said, 'seeing all the 'ole you've dug.'

"I was in a regular daze all dinner, wondering whether that chap next door wasn't over the fence and filling 'is pockets. But in the afternoon I got easier in my mind—it seemed to me it must 'ave been there so long it was pretty sure to stop a bit longer—and I tried to get up a bit of a discussion to dror out the old man and see what 'E thought of treasure trove."

Mr. Brisher paused, and affected amusement at the memory.

"The old man was a scorcher," he said; "a regular scorcher."

"What!" said I; "did he—?"

"It was like this," explained Mr. Brisher, laying a friendly hand on my arm and breathing into my face to calm me. "Just to dror 'im out, I told a story of a chap I said I knew—pretendin', you know—who'd found a sovring in a novercoat 'e'd borrowed. I said 'e stuck to it, but I said I wasn't sure whether that was right or not. And then the old man began. Lor'! 'e DID let me 'ave it!" Mr. Brisher affected an insincere amusement. "'E was, well—what you might call a rare 'and at Snacks. Said that was the sort of friend 'e'd naturally expect me to 'ave. Said 'e'd naturally expect that from the friend of a out-of-work loafer who took up with daughters who didn't belong to 'im. There! I couldn't tell you 'ARF 'e said. 'E went on most outrageous. I stood up to 'im about it, just to dror 'im out. 'Wouldn't you stick to a 'arf-sov', not if you found it in the street?' I says. 'Certainly not,' 'e says; 'certainly I wouldn't.' 'What! not if you found it as a sort of treasure?' 'Young man,' 'e says, 'there's 'i'er 'thority than mine—Render unto Caesar'—what is it? Yes. Well, he fetched up that. A rare 'and at 'itting you over the 'ed with the Bible, was the old man. And so he went on. 'E got to such Snacks about me at last I couldn't stand it. I'd promised Jane not to answer 'im back, but it got a bit TOO thick. I—I give it 'im...”

Mr. Brisher, by means of enigmatical facework, tried to make me think he had had the best of that argument, but I knew better.

"I went out in a 'uff at last. But not before I was pretty sure I 'ad to lift that treasure by myself. The only thing that kep' me up was thinking 'ow I'd take it out of 'im when I 'ad the cash."

There was a lengthy pause.

"Now, you'd 'ardly believe it, but all them three days I never 'ad a chance at the blessed treasure, never got out not even a 'arf-crown. There was always a Somethink—always.

"'Stonishing thing it isn't thought of more," said Mr. Brisher. "Finding treasure's no great shakes. It's gettin' it. I don't suppose I slep' a wink any of those nights, thinking where I was to take it, what I was to do with it, 'ow I was to explain it. It made me regular ill. And days I was that dull, it made Jane regular 'uffy. 'You ain't the same chap you was in London,' she says, several times. I tried to lay it on 'er father and 'is Snacks, but bless you, she knew better. What must she 'ave but that I'd got another girl on my mind! Said I wasn't True. Well, we had a bit of a row. But I was that set on the Treasure, I didn't seem to mind a bit Anything she said.

"Well, at last I got a sort of plan. I was always a bit good at planning, though carrying out isn't so much in my line. I thought it all out and settled on a plan. First, I was going to take all my pockets full of these 'ere 'arf-crowns—see?—and afterwards as I shall tell.

"Well, I got to that state I couldn't think of getting at the Treasure again in the daytime, so I waited until the night before I had to go, and then, when everything was still, up I gets and slips down to the back door, meaning to get my pockets full. What must I do in the scullery but fall over a pail! Up gets 'er father with a gun—'e was a light sleeper was 'er father, and very suspicious and there was me: 'ad to explain I'd come down to the pump for a drink because my water-bottle was bad. 'E didn't let me off a Snack or two over that bit, you lay a bob."

"And you mean to say—" I began.

"Wait a bit," said Mr. Brisher. "I say, I'd made my plan. That put the kybosh on one bit, but it didn't 'urt the general scheme not a bit. I went and I finished that rockery next day, as though there wasn't a Snack in the world; cemented over the stones, I did, dabbed it green and everythink. I put a dab of green just to show where the box was. They all came and looked at it, and sai 'ow nice it was—even 'e was a bit softer like to see it, and all he said was, 'It's a pity you can't always work like that, then you might get something definite to do,' he says.

"'Yes,' I says—I couldn't 'elp it—'I put a lot in that rockery,' I says, like that. See? 'I put a lot in that rockery'—meaning—"

"I see," said I—for Mr. Brisher is apt to overelaborate his jokes.

"'*E* didn't," said Mr. Brisher. "Not then, anyhow."

"Ar'ever—after all that was over, off I set for London.... Orf I set for London."

Pause.

"On'y I wasn't going to no London," said Mr. Brisher, with sudden animation, and thrusting his face into mine. "No fear! What do YOU think?

"I didn't go no further than Colchester—not a yard.

"I'd left the spade just where I could find it. I'd got everything planned and right. I 'ired a little trap in Colchester, and pretended I wanted to go to Ipswich and stop the night, and come back next day, and the chap I 'ired it from made me leave two sovrings on it right away, and off I set.

"I didn't go to no Ipswich neither.

"Midnight the 'orse and trap was 'itched by the little road that ran by the cottage where 'e lived—not sixty yards off, it wasn't—and I was at it like a good 'un. It was jest the night for such games—overcast—but a trifle too 'ot, and all round the sky there was summer lightning and presently a thunderstorm. Down it came. First big drops in a sort of fizzle, then 'ail. I kep'on. I whacked at it—I didn't dream the old man would 'ear. I didn't even trouble to go quiet with the spade, and the thunder and lightning and 'ail seemed to excite me like. I shouldn't wonder if I was singing. I got so 'ard at it I clean forgot the thunder and the 'orse and trap. I precious soon got the box showing, and started to lift it...."

"Heavy?" I said.

"I couldn't no more lift it than fly. I WAS sick. I'd never thought of that I got regular wild—I tell you, I cursed. I got sort of outrageous. I didn't think of dividing it like for the minute, and even then I couldn't 'ave took money about loose in a trap. I hoisted one end sort of wild like, and over the whole show went with a tremenjous noise. Perfeck smash of silver. And then right on the heels of that, Flash! Lightning like the day! and there was the back door open and the old man coming down the garden with 'is blooming old gun. He wasn't not a 'undred yards away!

"I tell you I was that upset—I didn't think what I was doing. I never stopped-not even to fill my pockets. I went over the fence like a shot, and ran like one o'clock for the trap, cussing and swearing as I went. I WAS in a state...."

"And will you believe me, when I got to the place where I'd left the 'orse and trap, they'd gone. Orf! When I saw that I 'adn't a cuss left for it. I jest danced on the grass, and when I'd danced enough I started off to London.... I was done."

Mr. Brisher was pensive for an interval. "I was done," he repeated, very bitterly.

"Well?" I said.

"That's all," said Mr. Brisher.

"You didn't go back?"

"No fear. I'd 'ad enough of THAT blooming treasure, any'ow for a bit. Besides, I didn't know what was done to chaps who tried to collar a treasure trove. I started off for London there and then...."

"And you never went back?"

"Never."

"But about Jane? Did you write?"

"Three times, fishing like. And no answer. We'd parted in a bit of a 'uff on account of 'er being jealous. So that I couldn't make out for certain what it meant.

"I didn't know what to do. I didn't even know whether the old man knew it was me. I sort of kep' an eye open on papers to see when he'd give up that treasure to the Crown, as I hadn't a doubt 'e would, considering 'ow respectable he'd always been."

"And did he?"

Mr. Brisher pursed his mouth and moved his head slowly from side to side. "Not 'IM," he said.

"Jane was a nice girl," he said, "a thorough nice girl mind you, if jealous, and there's no knowing I mightn't 'ave gone back to 'er after a bit. I thought if he didn't give up the treasure I might 'ave a sort of 'old on 'im.... Well, one day

I looks as usual under Colchester—and there I saw 'is name. What for, d'yer think?"

I could not guess.

Mr. Brisher's voice sank to a whisper, and once more he spoke behind his hand. His manner was suddenly suffused with a positive joy. "Issuing counterfeit coins," he said. "Counterfeit coins!"

"You don't mean to say—?"

"Yes-It. Bad. Quite a long case they made of it. But they got 'im, though he dodged tremenjous. Traced 'is 'aving passed, oh!—nearly a dozen bad 'arf-crowns."

"And you didn't—?"

"No fear. And it didn't do 'IM much good to say it was treasure trove."

12. MISS WINCHELSEA'S HEART

Miss Winchelsea was going to Rome. The matter had filled her mind for a month or more, and had overflowed so abundantly into her conversation that quite a number of people who were not going to Rome, and who were not likely to go to Rome, had made it a personal grievance against her. Some indeed had attempted quite unavailingly to convince her that Rome was not nearly such a desirable place as it was reported to be, and others had gone so far as to suggest behind her back that she was dreadfully "stuck up" about "that Rome of hers." And little Lily Hardhurst had told her friend Mr. Binns that so far as she was concerned Miss Winchelsea might "go to her old Rome and stop there; SHE (Miss Lily Hardhurst) wouldn't grieve." And the way in which Miss Winchelsea put herself upon terms of personal tenderness with Horace and Benvenuto Cellini and Raphael and Shelley and Keats—if she had been Shelley's widow she could not have professed a keener interest in his grave—was a matter of universal astonishment. Her dress was a triumph of tactful discretion, sensible, but not too "touristy"—Miss Winchelsea, had a great dread of being "touristy"—and her Baedeker was carried in a cover of grey to hide its glaring red. She made a prim and pleasant little figure on the Charing Cross platform, in spite of her swelling pride, when at last the great day dawned, and she could start for Rome. The day was bright, the Channel passage would be pleasant, and all the omens promised well. There was the gayest sense of adventure in this unprecedented departure.

She was going with two friends who had been fellow-students with her at the training college, nice honest girls both, though not so good at history and literature as Miss Winchelsea. They both looked up to her immensely, though physically they had to look down, and she anticipated some pleasant times to be spent in "stirring them up" to her own pitch of aesthetic and historical enthusiasm. They had secured seats already, and welcomed her effusively at the carriage door. In the instant criticism of the encounter she noted that Fanny had a slightly "touristy" leather strap, and that Helen had succumbed to a serge jacket with side pockets, into which her hands were thrust. But they were much too happy with themselves and the expedition for their friend to attempt any hint at the moment about these things. As soon as the first ecstasies were over—Fanny's enthusiasm was a little noisy and crude, and consisted mainly in emphatic repetitions of "Just FANCY! we're going to Rome, my dear!—Rome!"—they gave their attention to their fellow-travellers. Helen was anxious to secure a compartment to themselves, and, in order to discourage intruders, got out and planted herself firmly on the step. Miss Winchelsea peeped out over her shoulder, and made sly little remarks about the accumulating people on the platform, at which Fanny laughed gleefully.

They were travelling with one of Mr. Thomas Gunn's parties—fourteen days in Rome for fourteen pounds. They did not belong to the personally conducted party of course—Miss Winchelsea had seen to that—but they travelled with it because of the convenience of that arrangement. The people were the oddest mixture, and wonderfully amusing. There was a vociferous red-faced polyglot personal conductor in a pepper-and-salt suit, very long in the arms and legs and very active. He shouted proclamations. When he wanted to speak to people he stretched out an arm and held them until his purpose was accomplished. One hand was full of papers, tickets, counterfoils of tourists. The people of the personally conducted party were, it seemed, of two sorts; people the conductor wanted and could not find, and people he did not want and who followed him in a steadily growing tail up and down the platform. These people seemed, indeed, to think that their one chance of reaching Rome lay in keeping close to him. Three little old ladies were particularly energetic in his pursuit, and at last maddened him to the pitch of clapping them into a carriage and daring them to emerge again. For the rest of the time, one, two, or three of their heads protruded from the window wailing enquiries about "a little wickerwork box" whenever he drew near. There was a very stout man with a very stout wife in shiny black; there was a little old man like an aged hostler.

"What CAN such people want in Rome?" asked Miss Winchelsea. "What can it mean to them?" There was a very tall curate in a very small straw hat, and a very short curate encumbered by a long camera stand. The contrast amused Fanny very much. Once they heard some one calling for "Snooks." "I always thought that name was invented by novelists," said Miss Winchelsea. "Fancy! Snooks. I wonder which IS Mr. Snooks." Finally they picked out a very stout and resolute little man in a large check suit. "If he isn't Snooks, he ought to be," said Miss Winchelsea.

Presently the conductor discovered Helen's attempt at a corner in carriages. "Room for five," he bawled with a parallel translation on his fingers. A party of four together—mother, father, and two daughters—blundered in, all greatly excited. "It's all right, Ma, you let me," said one of the daughters, hitting her mother's bonnet with a handbag she struggled to put in the rack. Miss Winchelsea detested people who banged about and called their mother "Ma." A young man travelling alone followed. He was not at all "touristy" in his costume, Miss Winchelsea observed; his Gladstone bag was of good pleasant leather with labels reminiscent of Luxembourg and Ostend, and his boots, though brown, were not vulgar. He carried an overcoat on his arm. Before these people had properly settled in their places, came an inspection of tickets and a slamming of doors, and behold! they were gliding out of Charing Cross station on their way to Rome.

"Fancy!" cried Fanny, "we are going to Rome, my dear! Rome! I don't seem to believe it, even now."

Miss Winchelsea suppressed Fanny's emotions with a little smile, and the lady who was called "Ma" explained to people in general why they had "cut it so close" at the station. The two daughters called her "Ma" several times, toned her down in a tactless effective way, and drove her at last to the muttered inventory of a basket of travelling requisites. Presently she looked up. "Lor'!" she said, "I didn't bring THEM!" Both the daughters said "Oh, Ma!" but what "them" was did not appear. Presently Fanny produced Hare's Walks in Rome, a sort of mitigated guide-book very popular among Roman visitors; and the father of the two daughters began to examine his books of tickets minutely, apparently in a search after English words. When he had looked at the tickets for a long time right way up, he turned them upside down. Then he produced a fountain pen and dated them with considerable care. The young man, having completed an unostentatious survey of his fellow travellers, produced a book and fell to reading. When Helen and Fanny were looking out of the window at Chiselhurst—the place interested Fanny because the poor dear Empress of the French used to live there—Miss Winchelsea took the opportunity to observe the book the young man held. It was not a guide-book, but a little thin volume of poetry—BOUND. She glanced at his face—it seemed a refined pleasant face to her hasty glance. He wore a little gilt pince-nez. "Do you think she lives there now?" said Fanny, and Miss Winchelsea's inspection came to an end.

For the rest of the journey Miss Winchelsea talked little, and what she said was as pleasant and as stamped with refinement as she could make it. Her voice was always low and clear and pleasant, and she took care that on this occasion it was particularly low and clear and pleasant. As they came under the white cliffs the young man put his book of poetry away, and when at last the train stopped beside the boat, he displayed a graceful alacrity with the impedimenta of Miss Winchelsea and her friends. Miss Winchelsea hated nonsense, but she was pleased to see the young man perceived at once that they were ladies, and helped them without any violent geniality; and how nicely he showed that his civilities were to be no excuse for further intrusions. None of her little party had been out of England before, and they were all excited and a little nervous at the Channel passage. They stood in a little group in a good place near the middle of the boat—the young man had taken Miss Winchelsea's carry-all there and had told her it was a good place—and they watched the white shores of Albion recede and quoted Shakespeare and made quiet fun of their fellow travellers in the English way.

They were particularly amused at the precautions the bigger-sized people had taken against the little waves—cut lemons and flasks prevailed, one lady lay full-length in a deck chair with a handkerchief over her face, and a very broad resolute man in a bright brown "touristy" suit walked all the way from England to France along the deck, with his legs as widely apart as Providence permitted. These were all excellent precautions, and, nobody was ill. The personally conducted party pursued the conductor about the deck with enquiries in a manner that suggested to Helen's mind the rather vulgar image of hens with a piece of bacon peel, until at last he went into hiding below. And the young man with the thin volume of poetry stood at the stern watching England receding, looking rather lonely and sad to Miss Winchelsea's eye.

And then came Calais and tumultuous novelties, and the young man had not forgotten Miss Winchelsea's hold-all and the other little things. All three girls, though they had passed government examinations in French to any extent, were stricken with a dumb shame of their accents, and the young man was very useful. And he did not intrude. He put them in a comfortable carriage and raised his hat and went away. Miss Winchelsea thanked him in her best manner—a pleasing, cultivated manner—and Fanny said he was "nice" almost before he was out of earshot. "I wonder what he can be," said Helen. "He's going to Italy, because I noticed green tickets in his book." Miss Winchelsea almost told them of the poetry, and decided not to do so. And presently the carriage windows seized hold upon them and the young man was forgotten. It made them feel that they were doing an educated sort of thing to travel through a country whose commonest advertisements were in idiomatic French, and Miss Winchelsea made unpatriotic comparisons because there were weedy little sign-board advertisements by the rail side instead of the broad hoardings that deface the landscape in our land. But the north of France is really uninteresting country, and after a time Fanny reverted to Hare's Walks and Helen initiated lunch. Miss Winchelsea awoke out of a happy reverie; she had been trying to realise, she said, that she was actually going to Rome, but she perceived at Helen's suggestion that she was hungry, and they lunched out of their baskets very cheerfully. In the afternoon they were tired and silent until Helen made tea. Miss Winchelsea might have dozed, only she knew Fanny slept with her mouth open; and as their fellow passengers were two rather nice critical-looking ladies of uncertain age—who knew French well enough to talk it—she employed herself in keeping Fanny awake. The rhythm of the train became insistent, and the streaming landscape outside became at last quite painful to the eye. They were already dreadfully tired of travelling before their night's stoppage came.

The stoppage for the night was brightened by the appearance of the young man, and his manners were all that could be desired and his French quite serviceable. His coupons availed for the same hotel as theirs, and by chance as it seemed he sat next Miss Winchelsea at the table d'hote. In spite of her enthusiasm for Rome, she had thought out some such possibility very thoroughly, and when he ventured to make a remark upon the tediousness of travelling—he let the soup and fish go by before he did this—she did not simply assent to his proposition, but responded with another. They were soon comparing their journeys, and Helen and Fanny were cruelly overlooked in the conversation. It was to be the same journey, they found; one day for the galleries at Florence—"from what I hear," said the young man, "it is barely enough,"—and the rest at Rome. He talked of Rome very pleasantly; he was evidently quite well read, and he quoted Horace about Soracte. Miss Winchelsea had "done" that book of Horace for her matriculation, and was delighted to cap his quotation. It gave a sort of tone to things, this incident—a touch of refinement to mere chatting. Fanny expressed a few emotions, and Helen interpolated a few sensible remarks, but the bulk of the talk on the girls' side naturally fell to Miss Winchelsea.

Before they reached Rome this young man was tacitly of their party. They did not know his name nor what he was, but it seemed he taught, and Miss Winchelsea had a shrewd idea he was an extension lecturer. At any rate he was something of that sort, something gentlemanly and refined without being opulent and impossible. She tried once or twice to ascertain whether he came from Oxford or Cambridge, but he missed her timid importunities. She tried to get him to make remarks about those places to see if he would say "come up" to them instead of "go down"—she knew that was how you told a 'Varsity man. He used the word "Varsity"—not university—in quite the proper way.

They saw as much of Mr. Ruskin's Florence as the brief time permitted; he met them in the Pitti Gallery and went round with them, chatting brightly, and evidently very grateful for their recognition. He knew a great deal about art, and all four enjoyed the morning immensely. It was fine to go round recognising old favourites and finding new beauties, especially while so many people fumbled helplessly with Baedeker. Nor was he a bit of a prig, Miss Winchelsea said, and indeed she detested prigs. He had a distinct undertone of humour, and was funny, for example, without being vulgar, at the expense of the quaint work of Beato Angelico. He had a grave seriousness beneath it all, and was quick to seize the moral lessons of the pictures. Fanny went softly among these masterpieces; she admitted "she knew so little about them," and she confessed that to her they were "all beautiful." Fanny's "beautiful" inclined to be a little monotonous, Miss Winchelsea thought. She had been quite glad when the last sunny Alp had vanished, because of the staccato of Fanny's admiration. Helen said little, but Miss Winchelsea had found her a little wanting on the aesthetic side in the old days and was not surprised; sometimes she laughed at the young man's hesitating delicate little jests and sometimes she didn't, and sometimes she seemed quite lost to the art about them in the contemplation of the dresses of the other visitors.

At Rome the young man was with them intermittently. A rather "touristy" friend of his took him away at times. He complained comically to Miss Winchelsea. "I have only two short weeks in Rome," he said, "and my friend Leonard wants to spend a whole day at Tivoli, looking at a waterfall."

"What is your friend Leonard?" asked Miss Winchelsea abruptly.

"He's the most enthusiastic pedestrian I ever met," the young man replied, amusingly, but a little unsatisfactorily, Miss Winchelsea thought. They had some glorious times, and Fanny could not think what they would have done without him. Miss Winchelsea's interest and Fanny's enormous capacity for admiration were insatiable. They never flagged—through pictures and sculpture galleries, immense crowded churches, ruins and museums, Judas trees and prickly pears, wine carts and palaces, they admired their way unflinchingly. They never saw a stone pine or a eucalyptus but they named and admired it; they never glimpsed Soracte but they exclaimed. Their common ways were made wonderful by imaginative play. "Here Caesar may have walked," they would say. "Raphael may have seen Soracte from this very point." They happened on the tomb of Bibulus. "Old Bibulus," said the young man. "The oldest monument of Republican Rome!" said Miss Winchelsea.

"I'm dreadfully stupid," said Fanny, "but who WAS Bibulus?"

There was a curious little pause.

"Wasn't he the person who built the wall?" said Helen.

The young man glanced quickly at her and laughed. "That was Balbus," he said. Helen reddened, but neither he nor Miss Winchelsea threw any light upon Fanny's ignorance about Bibulus.

Helen was more taciturn than the other three, but then she was always taciturn, and usually she took care of the tram tickets and things like that, or kept her eye on them if the young man took them, and told him where they were when he wanted them. Glorious times they had, these young people, in that pale brown cleanly city of memories that was once the world. Their only sorrow was the shortness of the time. They said indeed that the electric trams and the '70 buildings, and that criminal advertisement that glares upon the Forum, outraged their aesthetic feelings unspeakably; but that was only part of the fun. And indeed Rome is such a wonderful place that it made Miss Winchelsea forget some of her most carefully prepared enthusiasms at times, and Helen, taken unawares, would suddenly admit the beauty of unexpected things. Yet Fanny and Helen would have liked a shop window or so in the

English quarter if Miss Winchelsea's uncompromising hostility to all other English visitors had not rendered that district impossible.

The intellectual and aesthetic fellowship of Miss Winchelsea and the scholarly young man passed insensibly towards a deeper feeling. The exuberant Fanny did her best to keep pace with their recondite admiration by playing her "beautiful," with vigour, and saying "Oh! LET'S go," with enormous appetite whenever a new place of interest was mentioned. But Helen developed a certain want of sympathy towards the end, that disappointed Miss Winchelsea a little. She refused to "see anything" in the face of Beatrice Cenci—Shelley's Beatrice Cenci!—in the Barberini gallery; and one day, when they were deploring the electric trams, she said rather snappishly that "people must get about somehow, and it's better than torturing horses up these horrid little hills." She spoke of the Seven Hills of Rome as "horrid little hills!"

And the day they went on the Palatine—though Miss Winchelsea did not know of this—she remarked suddenly to Fanny, "Don't hurry like that, my dear; THEY don't want us to overtake them. And we don't say the right things for them when we DO get near."

"I wasn't trying to overtake them," said Fanny, slackening her excessive pace; "I wasn't indeed." And for a minute she was short of breath.

But Miss Winchelsea had come upon happiness. It was only when she came to look back across an intervening tragedy that she quite realised how happy she had been, pacing among the cypress-shadowed ruins, and exchanging the very highest class of information the human mind can possess, the most refined impressions it is possible to convey. Insensibly emotion crept into their intercourse, sunning itself openly and pleasantly at last when Helen's modernity was not too near. Insensibly their interest drifted from the wonderful associations about them to their more intimate and personal feelings. In a tentative way information was supplied; she spoke allusively of her school, of her examination successes, of her gladness that the days of "Cram" were over. He made it quite clear that he also was a teacher. They spoke of the greatness of their calling, of the necessity of sympathy to face its irksome details, of a certain loneliness they sometimes felt.

That was in the Colosseum, and it was as far as they got that day, because Helen returned with Fanny—she had taken her into the upper galleries. Yet the private dreams of Miss Winchelsea, already vivid and concrete enough, became now realistic in the highest degree. She figured that pleasant young man, lecturing in the most edifying way to his students, herself modestly prominent as his intellectual mate and helper; she figured a refined little home, with two bureaus, with white shelves of high-class books, and autotypes of the pictures of Rossetti and Burne-Jones, with Morris's wall papers and flowers in pots of beaten copper. Indeed she figured many things. On the Pincio the two had a few precious moments together, while Helen marched Fanny off to see the muro Torto, and he spoke at once plainly. He said he hoped their friendship was only beginning, that he already found her company very precious to him, that indeed it was more than that.

He became nervous, thrusting at his glasses with trembling fingers as though he fancied his emotions made them unstable. "I should of course," he said, "tell you things about myself. I know it is rather unusual my speaking to you like this. Only our meeting has been so accidental—or providential—and I am snatching at things. I came to Rome expecting a lonely tour... and I have been so very happy, so very happy. Quite recently I found myself in a position—I have dared to think—. And—"

He glanced over his shoulder and stopped. He said "Damn!" quite distinctly—and she did not condemn him for that manly lapse into profanity. She looked and saw his friend Leonard advancing. He drew nearer; he raised his hat to Miss Winchelsea, and his smile was almost a grin. "I've been looking for you everywhere, Snooks," he said. "You promised to be on the Piazza steps half an hour ago."

Snooks! The name struck Miss Winchelsea like a blow in the face. She did not hear his reply. She thought afterwards that Leonard must have considered her the vaguest-minded person. To this day she is not sure whether she was introduced to Leonard or not, nor what she said to him. A sort of mental paralysis was upon her. Of all offensive surnames—Snooks!

Helen and Fanny were returning, there were civilities, and the young men were receding. By a great effort she controlled herself to face the enquiring eyes of her friends. All that afternoon she lived the life of a heroine under the indescribable outrage of that name, chatting, observing, with "Snooks" gnawing at her heart. From the moment that it first rang upon her ears, the dream of her happiness was prostrate in the dust. All the refinement she had figured was ruined and defaced by that cognomen's unavoidable vulgarity.

What was that refined little home to her now, spite of autotypes, Morris papers, and bureaus? Athwart it in letters of fire ran an incredible inscription: "Mrs. Snooks." That may seem a little thing to the reader, but consider the delicate refinement of Miss Winchelsea's mind. Be as refined as you can and then think of writing yourself down:—"Snooks." She conceived herself being addressed as Mrs. Snooks by all the people she liked least, conceived the patronymic touched with a vague quality of insult. She figured a card of grey and silver bearing "Winchelsea," triumphantly effaced by an arrow, Cupid's arrow, in favour of "Snooks." Degrading confession of feminine weakness! She imagined the terrible rejoicings of certain girl friends, of certain grocer cousins from whom her growing refinement had long since estranged her. How they would make it sprawl across the envelope that would bring their sarcastic congratulations. Would even his pleasant company compensate her for that? "It is impossible," she muttered; "impossible! SNOOKS!"

She was sorry for him, but not so sorry as she was for herself. For him she had a touch of indignation. To be so nice, so refined, while all the time he was "Snooks," to hide under a pretentious gentility of demeanour the badge sinister of his surname seemed a sort of treachery. To put it in the language of sentimental science she felt he had "led her on."

There were of course moments of terrible vacillation, a period even when something almost like passion bid her throw refinement to the winds. And there was something in her, an unexpurgated vestige of vulgarity, that made a strenuous attempt at proving that Snooks was not so very bad a name after all. Any hovering hesitation flew before Fanny's manner, when Fanny came with an air of catastrophe to tell that she also knew the horror. Fanny's voice fell to a whisper when she said SNOOKS. Miss Winchelsea would not give him any answer when at last, in the Borghese, she could have a minute with him; but she promised him a note.

She handed him that note in the little book of poetry he had lent her, the little book that had first drawn them together. Her refusal was ambiguous, allusive. She could no more tell him why she rejected him than she could have told a cripple of his hump. He too must feel something of the unspeakable quality of his name. Indeed he had avoided a dozen chances of telling it, she now perceived. So she spoke of "obstacles she could not reveal"—"reasons why the thing he spoke of was impossible." She addressed the note with a shiver, "E. K. Snooks."

Things were worse than she had dreaded; he asked her to explain. How COULD she explain? Those last two days in Rome were dreadful. She was haunted by his air of astonished perplexity. She knew she had given him intimate hopes, she had not the courage to examine her mind thoroughly for the extent of her encouragement. She knew he must think her the most changeable of beings. Now that she was in full retreat, she would not even perceive his hints of a possible correspondence. But in that matter he did a thing that seemed to her at once delicate and romantic. He made a go-between of Fanny. Fanny could not keep the secret, and came and told her that night under a transparent pretext of needed advice. "Mr. Snooks," said Fanny, "wants to write to me. Fancy! I had no idea. But should I let him?" They talked it over long and earnestly, and Miss Winchelsea was careful to keep the veil over her heart. She was already repenting his disregarded hints. Why should she not hear of him sometimes—painful though his name must be to her? Miss Winchelsea decided it might be permitted, and Fanny kissed her good-night with unusual emotion. After she had gone Miss Winchelsea sat for a long time at the window of her little room. It was moonlight, and down the street a man sang "Santa Lucia" with almost heart-dissolving tenderness.... She sat very still.

She breathed a word very softly to herself. The word was "SNOOKS." Then she got up with a profound sigh, and went to bed. The next morning he said to her meaningly, "I shall hear of you through your friend."

Mr. Snooks saw them off from Rome with that pathetic interrogative perplexity still on his face, and if it had not been for Helen he would have retained Miss Winchelsea's hold-all in his hand as a sort of encyclopaedic keepsake. On their way back to England Miss Winchelsea on six separate occasions made Fanny promise to write to her the longest of long letters. Fanny, it seemed, would be quite near Mr. Snooks. Her new school—she was always going to new schools—would be only five miles from Steely Bank, and it was in the Steely Bank Polytechnic, and one or two first-class schools, that Mr. Snooks did his teaching. He might even see her at times. They could not talk much of him—she and Fanny always spoke of "him," never of Mr. Snooks,—because Helen was apt to say unsympathetic things about him. Her nature had coarsened very much, Miss Winchelsea perceived, since the old Training College days; she had become hard and cynical. She thought he had a weak face, mistaking refinement for weakness as people of her stamp are apt to do, and when she heard his name was Snooks, she said she had expected something of the sort. Miss Winchelsea was careful to spare her own feelings after that, but Fanny was less circumspect.

The girls parted in London, and Miss Winchelsea returned, with a new interest in life, to the Girls' High School in which she had been an increasingly valuable assistant for the last three years. Her new interest in life was Fanny as a correspondent, and to give her a lead she wrote her a lengthy descriptive letter within a fortnight of her return. Fanny answered, very disappointingly. Fanny indeed had no literary gift, but it was new to Miss Winchelsea to find herself deploring the want of gifts in a friend. That letter was even criticised aloud in the safe solitude of Miss Winchelsea's study, and her criticism, spoken with great bitterness, was "Twaddle!" It was full of just the things Miss Winchelsea's letter had been full of, particulars of the school. And of Mr. Snooks, only this much: "I have had a letter from Mr. Snooks, and he has been over to see me on two Saturday afternoons running. He talked about Rome and you; we both talked about you. Your ears must have burnt, my dear...."

Miss Winchelsea repressed a desire to demand more explicit information, and wrote the sweetest long letter again. "Tell me all about yourself, dear. That journey has quite refreshed our ancient friendship, and I do so want to keep in touch with you." About Mr. Snooks she simply wrote on the fifth page that she was glad Fanny had seen him, and that if he SHOULD ask after her, she was to be remembered to him VERY KINDLY (underlined). And Fanny replied most obtusely in the key of that "ancient friendship," reminding Miss Winchelsea of a dozen foolish things of those old schoolgirl days at the training college, and saying not a word about Mr. Snooks!

For nearly a week Miss Winchelsea was so angry at the failure of Fanny as a go-between that she could not write to her. And then she wrote less effusively, and in her letter she asked point-blank, "Have you seen Mr. Snooks?" Fanny's letter was unexpectedly satisfactory. "I HAVE seen Mr. Snooks," she wrote, and having once named him she kept on about him; it was all Snooks—Snooks this and Snooks that. He was to give a public lecture, said Fanny, among other things. Yet Miss Winchelsea, after the first glow of gratification, still found this letter a little unsatisfactory. Fanny did not report Mr. Snooks as saying anything about Miss Winchelsea, nor as looking a little white and worn, as he ought to have been doing. And behold! before she had replied, came a second letter from Fanny on the same theme, quite a gushing letter, and covering six sheets with her loose feminine hand.

And about this second letter was a rather odd little thing that Miss Winchelsea only noticed as she re-read it the third time. Fanny's natural femininity had prevailed even against the round and clear traditions of the training college; she was one of those she-creatures born to make all her m's and n's and u's and r's and e's alike, and to leave her o's and a's open and her i's undotted. So that it was only after an elaborate comparison of word with word that Miss Winchelsea felt assured Mr. Snooks was not really "Mr. Snooks" at all! In Fanny's first letter of gush he was Mr. "Snooks," in her second the spelling was changed to Mr. "Senoks." Miss Winchelsea's hand positively trembled as she turned the sheet over—it meant so much to her. For it had already begun to seem to her that even the name of Mrs. Snooks might be avoided at too great a price, and suddenly—this possibility! She turned over the six sheets, all dappled with that critical name, and everywhere the first letter had the form of an E! For a time she walked the room with a hand pressed upon her heart.

She spent a whole day pondering this change, weighing a letter of inquiry that should be at once discreet and effectual, weighing too what action she should take after the answer came. She was resolved that if this altered spelling was anything more than a quaint fancy of Fanny's, she would write forthwith to Mr. Snooks. She had now reached a stage when the minor refinements of behaviour disappear. Her excuse remained uninvented, but she had the subject of her letter clear in her mind, even to the hint that "circumstances in my life have changed very greatly since we talked together." But she never gave that hint. There came a third letter from that fitful correspondent Fanny. The first line proclaimed her "the happiest girl alive."

Miss Winchelsea crushed the letter in her hand—the rest unread—and sat with her face suddenly very still. She had received it just before morning school, and had opened it when the junior mathematicians were well under way. Presently she resumed reading with an appearance of great calm. But after the first sheet she went on reading the third without discovering the error:—"told him frankly I did not like his name," the third sheet began. "He told me he did not like it himself—you know that sort of sudden frank way he has"—Miss Winchelsea did know. "So I said 'Couldn't you change it?' He didn't see it at first. Well, you know, dear, he had told me what it really meant; it means Sevenoaks, only it has got down to Snooks—both Snooks and Noaks, dreadfully vulgar surnames though they be, are really worn forms of Sevenoaks. So I said—even I have my bright ideas at times—'if it got down from Sevenoaks to Snooks, why not get it back from Snooks to Sevenoaks?' And the long and the short of it is, dear, he couldn't refuse me, and he changed his spelling there and then to Senoks for the bills of the new lecture. And afterwards, when we are married, we shall put in the apostrophe and make it Se'noks. Wasn't it kind of him to mind that fancy of mine, when many men would have taken offence? But it is just like him all over; he is as kind as he is clever. Because he knew as well as I did that I would have had him in spite of it, had he been ten times Snooks. But he did it all the same."

The class was startled by the sound of paper being viciously torn, and looked up to see Miss Winchelsea white in the face, and with some very small pieces of paper clenched in one hand. For a few seconds they stared at her stare, and then her expression changed back to a more familiar one. "Has any one finished number three?" she asked in an even tone. She remained calm after that. But impositions ruled high that day. And she spent two laborious evenings writing letters of various sorts to Fanny, before she found a decent congratulatory vein. Her reason struggled hopelessly against the persuasion that Fanny had behaved in an exceedingly treacherous manner.

One may be extremely refined and still capable of a very sore heart. Certainly Miss Winchelsea's heart was very sore. She had moods of sexual hostility, in which she generalised uncharitably about mankind. "He forgot himself with me," she said. "But Fanny is pink and pretty and soft and a fool—a very excellent match for a Man." And by way of a wedding present she sent Fanny a gracefully bound volume of poetry by George Meredith, and Fanny wrote back a grossly happy letter to say that it was "ALL beautiful." Miss Winchelsea hoped that some day Mr. Senoks might take up that slim book and think for a moment of the donor. Fanny wrote several times before and about her marriage, pursuing that fond legend of their "ancient friendship," and giving her happiness in the fullest detail. And Miss Winchelsea wrote to

Helen for the first time after the Roman journey, saying nothing about the marriage, but expressing very cordial feelings.

They had been in Rome at Easter, and Fanny was married in the August vacation. She wrote a garrulous letter to Miss Winchelsea, describing her home-coming, and the astonishing arrangements of their "teeny weeny" little house. Mr. Se'noks was now beginning to assume a refinement in Miss Winchelsea's memory out of all proportion to the facts of the case, and she tried in vain to imagine his cultured greatness in a "teeny weeny" little house. "Am busy enamelling a cosey corner," said Fanny, sprawling to the end of her third sheet, "so excuse more." Miss Winchelsea answered in her best style, gently poking fun at Fanny's arrangements and hoping intensely that Mr. Sen'oks might see the letter. Only this hope enabled her to write at all, answering not only that letter but one in November and one at Christmas.

The two latter communications contained urgent invitations for her to come to Steely Bank on a Visit during the Christmas holidays. She tried to think that HE had told her to ask that, but it was too much like Fanny's opulent good-nature. She could not but believe that he must be sick of his blunder by this time; and she had more than a hope that he would presently write her a letter beginning "Dear Friend." Something subtly tragic in the separation was a great support to her, a sad misunderstanding. To have been jilted would have been intolerable. But he never wrote that letter beginning "Dear Friend."

For two years Miss Winchelsea could not go to see her friends, in spite of the reiterated invitations of Mrs. Sevenoaks—it became full Sevenoaks in the second year. Then one day near the Easter rest she felt lonely and without a soul to understand her in the world, and her mind ran once more on what is called Platonic friendship. Fanny was clearly happy and busy in her new sphere of domesticity, but no doubt HE had his lonely hours. Did he ever think of those days in Rome—gone now beyond recalling? No one had understood her as he had done; no one in all the world. It would be a sort of melancholy pleasure to talk to him again, and what harm could it do? Why should she deny herself? That night she wrote a sonnet, all but the last two lines of the octave—which would not come, and the next day she composed a graceful little note to tell Fanny she was coming down.

And so she saw him again.

Even at the first encounter it was evident he had changed; he seemed stouter and less nervous, and it speedily appeared that his conversation had already lost much of its old delicacy. There even seemed a justification for Helen's description of weakness in his face—in certain lights it WAS weak. He seemed busy and preoccupied about his affairs, and almost under the impression that Miss Winchelsea had come for the sake of Fanny. He discussed his dinner with Fanny in an intelligent way. They only had one good long talk together, and that came to nothing. He did not refer to Rome, and spent some time abusing a man who had stolen an idea he had had for a text-book. It did not seem a very wonderful idea to Miss Winchelsea. She discovered he had forgotten the names of more than half the painters whose work they had rejoiced over in Florence.

It was a sadly disappointing week, and Miss Winchelsea was glad when it came to an end. Under various excuses she avoided visiting them again. After a time the visitor's room was occupied by their two little boys, and Fanny's invitations ceased. The intimacy of her letters had long since faded away.

13. A DREAM OF ARMAGEDDON

The man with the white face entered the carriage at Rugby. He moved slowly in spite of the urgency of his porter, and even while he was still on the platform I noted how ill he seemed. He dropped into the corner over against me with a sigh, made an incomplete attempt to arrange his travelling shawl, and became motionless, with his eyes staring vacantly. Presently he was moved by a sense of my observation, looked up at me, and put out a spiritless hand for his newspaper. Then he glanced again in my direction.

I feigned to read. I feared I had unwittingly embarrassed him, and in a moment I was surprised to find him speaking.

"I beg your pardon?" said I.

"That book," he repeated, pointing a lean finger, "is about dreams."

"Obviously," I answered, for it was Fortnum-Roscoe's Dream States, and the title was on the cover. He hung silent for a space as if he sought words. "Yes," he said at last, "but they tell you nothing." I did not catch his meaning for a second.

"They don't know," he added.

I looked a little more attentively at his face.

"There are dreams," he said, "and dreams."

That sort of proposition I never dispute.

"I suppose—" he hesitated. "Do you ever dream? I mean vividly."

"I dream very little," I answered. "I doubt if I have three vivid dreams in a year."

"Ah!" he said, and seemed for a moment to collect his thoughts.

"Your dreams don't mix with your memories?" he asked abruptly. "You don't find yourself in doubt; did this happen or did it not?"

"Hardly ever. Except just for a momentary hesitation now and then. I suppose few people do."

"Does HE say—" he indicated the book.

"Says it happens at times and gives the usual explanation about intensity of impression and the like to account for its not happening as a rule. I suppose you know something of these theories—"

"Very little—except that they are wrong."

His emaciated hand played with the strap of the window for a time. I prepared to resume reading, and that seemed to precipitate his next remark. He leant forward almost as though he would touch me.

"Isn't there something called consecutive dreaming—that goes on night after night?"

"I believe there is. There are cases given in most books on mental trouble."

"Mental trouble! Yes. I dare say there are. It's the right place for them. But what I mean—" He looked at his bony knuckles. "Is that sort of thing always dreaming? IS it dreaming? Or is it something else? Mightn't it be something else?"

I should have snubbed his persistent conversation but for the drawn anxiety of his face. I remember now the look of his faded eyes and the lids red-stained—perhaps you know that look.

"I'm not just arguing about a matter of opinion," he said. "The thing's killing me."

"Dreams?"

"If you call them dreams. Night after night. Vivid!—so vivid... this—" (he indicated the landscape that went streaming by the window) "seems unreal in comparison! I can scarcely remember who I am, what business I am on...."

He paused. "Even now—"

"The dream is always the same—do you mean?" I asked.

"It's over."

"You mean?"

"I died."

"Died?"

"Smashed and killed, and now, so much of me as that dream was, is dead. Dead for ever. I dreamt I was another man, you know, living in a different part of the world and in a different time. I dreamt that night after night. Night after night I woke into that other life. Fresh scenes and fresh happenings—until I came upon the last—"

"When you died?"

"When I died."

"And since then—"

"No," he said. "Thank God! That was the end of the dream...."

It was clear I was in for this dream. And after all, I had an hour before me, the light was fading fast, and Fortnum-Roscoe has a dreary way with him. "Living in a different time," I said: "do you mean in some different age?"

"Yes."

"Past?"

"No, to come—to come."

"The year three thousand, for example?"

"I don't know what year it was. I did when I was asleep, when I was dreaming, that is, but not now—not now that I am awake. There's a lot of things I have forgotten since I woke out of these dreams, though I knew them at the time when I was—I suppose it was dreaming. They called the year differently from our way of calling the year.... What DID they call it?" He put his hand to his forehead. "No," said he, "I forget."

He sat smiling weakly. For a moment I feared he did not mean to tell me his dream. As a rule I hate people who tell their dreams, but this struck me differently. I proffered assistance even. "It began—" I suggested.

"It was vivid from the first. I seemed to wake up in it suddenly. And it's curious that in these dreams I am speaking of I never remembered this life I am living now. It seemed as if the dream life was enough while it lasted. Perhaps—But I will tell you how I find myself when I do my best to recall it all. I don't remember anything dearly until I found myself sitting in a sort of loggia looking out over the sea. I had been dozing, and suddenly I woke up—fresh and vivid—not a bit dream-like—because the girl had stopped fanning me."

"The girl?"

"Yes, the girl. You must not interrupt or you will put me out."

He stopped abruptly. "You won't think I'm mad?" he said.

"No," I answered; "you've been dreaming. Tell me your dream."

"I woke up, I say, because the girl had stopped fanning me. I was not surprised to find myself there or anything of that sort, you understand. I did not feel I had fallen into it suddenly. I simply took it up at that point. Whatever memory I had of THIS life, this nineteenth-century life, faded as I woke, vanished like a dream. I knew all about myself, knew that my name was no longer Cooper but Hedon, and all about my position in the world. I've forgotten a lot since I woke—there's a want of connection—but it was all quite clear and matter of fact then."

He hesitated again, gripping the window strap, putting his face forward and looking up at me appealingly.

"This seems bosh to you?"

"No, no!" I cried. "Go on. Tell me what this loggia was like."

"It was not really a loggia—I don't know what to call it. It faced south. It was small. It was all in shadow except the semicircle above the balcony that showed the sky and sea and the corner where the girl stood. I was on a couch—it was a metal couch with light striped cushions-and the girl was leaning over the balcony with her back to me. The light of the sunrise fell on her ear and cheek. Her pretty white neck and the little curls that nestled there, and her white shoulder were in the sun, and all the grace of her body was in the cool blue shadow. She was dressed—how can I describe it? It was easy and flowing. And altogether there she stood, so that it came to me how beautiful and desirable she was, as though I had never seen her before. And when at last I sighed and raised myself upon my arm she turned her face to me—"

He stopped.

"I have lived three-and-fifty years in this world. I have had mother, sisters, friends, wife, and daughters—all their faces, the play of their faces, I know. But the face of this girl—it is much more real to me. I can bring it back into memory so that I see it again—I could draw it or paint it. And after all—"

He stopped—but I said nothing.

"The face of a dream—the face of a dream. She was beautiful. Not that beauty which is terrible, cold, and worshipful, like the beauty of a saint; nor that beauty that stirs fierce passions; but a sort of radiation, sweet lips that softened into smiles, and grave grey eyes. And she moved gracefully, she seemed to have part with all pleasant and gracious things—"

He stopped, and his face was downcast and hidden. Then he looked up at me and went on, making no further attempt to disguise his absolute belief in the reality of his story.

"You see, I had thrown up my plans and ambitions, thrown up all I had ever worked for or desired for her sake. I had been a master man away there in the north, with influence and property and a great reputation, but none of it had seemed worth having beside her. I had come to the place, this city of sunny pleasures, with her, and left all those things to wreck and ruin just to save a remnant at least of my life. While I had been in love with her before I knew that she had any care for me, before I had imagined that she would dare—that we should dare, all my life had seemed vain and hollow, dust and ashes. It WAS dust and ashes. Night after night and through the long days I had longed and desired—my soul had beaten against the thing forbidden!

"But it is impossible for one man to tell another just these things. It's emotion, it's a tint, a light that comes and goes. Only while it's there, everything changes, everything. The thing is I came away and left them in their Crisis to do what they could."

"Left whom?" I asked, puzzled.

"The people up in the north there. You see—in this dream, anyhow—I had been a big man, the sort of man men come to trust in, to group themselves about. Millions of men who had never seen me were ready to do things and risk things because of their confidence in me. I had been playing that game for years, that big laborious game, that vague, monstrous political game amidst intrigues and betrayals, speech and agitation. It was a vast weltering world, and at last I had a sort of leadership against the Gang—you know it was called the Gang—a sort of compromise of scoundrelly projects and base ambitions and vast public emotional stupidities and catchwords—the Gang that kept the world noisy and blind year by year, and all the while that it was drifting, drifting towards infinite disaster. But I can't expect you to understand the shades and complications of the year—the year something or other ahead. I had it all down to the smallest details—in my dream. I suppose I had been dreaming of it before I awoke, and the fading outline of some queer new development I had imagined still hung about me as I rubbed my eyes. It was some grubby affair that made me thank God for the sunlight. I sat up on the couch and remained looking at the woman and rejoicing—rejoicing that I had come away out of all that tumult and folly and violence before it was too late. After all, I thought, this is life—love and beauty, desire and delight, are they not worth all those dismal struggles for vague, gigantic ends? And I blamed myself for having ever sought to be a leader when I might have given my days to love. But then, thought I, if I had not spent my early days sternly and austerely, I might have wasted myself upon vain and worthless women, and at the thought all my being went out in love and tenderness to my dear mistress, my dear lady, who had come at last and compelled me—compelled me by her invincible charm for me—to lay that life aside.

"'You are worth it,' I said, speaking without intending her to hear; 'you are worth it, my dearest one; worth pride and praise and all things. Love! to have YOU is worth them all together.' And at the murmur of my voice she turned about.

"'Come and see,' she cried—I can hear her now—'come and see the sunrise upon Monte Solaro.'

"I remember how I sprang to my feet and joined her at the balcony. She put a white hand upon my shoulder and pointed towards great masses of limestone, flushing, as it were, into life. I looked. But first I noted the sunlight on her face caressing the lines of her cheeks and neck. How can I describe to you the scene we had before us? We were at Capri—"

"I have been there," I said. "I have clambered up Monte Solaro and drunk vero Capri—muddy stuff like cider—at the summit."

"Ah!" said the man with the white face; "then perhaps you can tell me—you will know if this was indeed Capri. For in this life I have never been there. Let me describe it. We were in a little room, one of a vast multitude of little rooms, very cool and sunny, hollowed out of the limestone of a sort of cape, very high above the sea. The whole island, you know, was one enormous hotel, complex beyond explaining, and on the other side there were miles of floating hotels, and huge floating stages to which the flying machines came. They called it a pleasure city. Of course, there was none of that in your time rather, I should say, IS none of that NOW. Of course. Now!—yes.

"Well, this room of ours was at the extremity of the cape, so that one could see east and west. Eastward was a great cliff—a thousand feet high perhaps— coldly grey except for one bright edge of gold, and beyond it the Isle of the Sirens, and a falling coast that faded and passed into the hot sunrise. And when one turned to the west, distinct and near was a little bay, a little beach still in shadow. And out of that shadow rose Solaro straight and tall, flushed and golden crested, like a beauty throned, and the white moon was floating behind her in the sky. And before us from east to west stretched the many-tinted sea all dotted with little sailing boats.

"To the eastward, of course, these little boats were grey and very minute and clear, but to the westward they were little boats of gold—shining gold— almost like little flames. And just below us was a rock with an arch worn through it. The blue sea-water broke to green and foam all round the rock, and a galley came gliding out of the arch."

"I know that rock," I said. "I was nearly drowned there. It is called the Faraglioni."

"I Faraglioni? Yes, she called it that," answered the man with the white face. "There was some story—but that—"

He put his hand to his forehead again. "No," he said, "I forget that story."

"Well, that is the first thing I remember, the first dream I had, that little shaded room and the beautiful air and sky and that dear lady of mine, with her shining arms and her graceful robe, and how we sat and talked in half whispers to one another. We talked in whispers not because there was any one to hear, but because there was still such a freshness of mind between us that our thoughts were a little frightened, I think, to find themselves at last in words. And so they went softly.

"Presently we were hungry and we went from our apartment, going by a strange passage with a moving floor, until we came to the great breakfast room—there was a fountain and music. A pleasant and joyful place it was, with its sunlight and splashing, and the murmur of plucked strings. And we sat and ate and smiled at one another, and I would not heed a man who was watching me from a table near by.

"And afterwards we went on to the dancing-hall. But I cannot describe that hall. The place was enormous—larger than any building you have ever seen—and in one place there was the old gate of Capri, caught into the wall of a gallery high overhead. Light girders, stems and threads of gold, burst from the pillars like fountains, streamed like an Aurora across the roof and interlaced, like—like conjuring tricks. All about the great circle for the dancers there were beautiful figures, strange dragons, and intricate and wonderful grotesques bearing lights. The place was inundated with artificial light that shamed the newborn day. And as we went through the throng the people turned about and looked at us, for all through the world my name and face were known, and how I had suddenly thrown up pride and struggle to come to this place. And they looked also at the lady beside me, though half the story of how at last she had come to me was unknown or mistold. And few of the men who were there, I know, but judged me a happy man, in spite of all the shame and dishonour that had come upon my name.

"The air was full of music, full of harmonious scents, full of the rhythm of beautiful motions. Thousands of beautiful people swarmed about the hall, crowded the galleries, sat in a myriad recesses; they were dressed in splendid colours and crowned with flowers; thousands danced about the great circle beneath the white images of the ancient gods, and glorious processions of youths and maidens came and went. We two danced, not the dreary monotonies of your days—of this time, I mean—but dances that were beautiful, intoxicating. And even now I can see my lady dancing—dancing joyously. She danced, you know, with a serious face; she danced with a serious dignity, and yet she was smiling at me and caressing me—smiling and caressing with her eyes.

"The music was different," he murmured. "It went—I cannot describe it; but it was infinitely richer and more varied than any music that has ever come to me awake.

"And then—it was when we had done dancing—a man came to speak to me. He was a lean, resolute man, very soberly clad for that place, and already I had marked his face watching me in the breakfasting hall, and afterwards as we went along the passage I had avoided his eye. But now, as we sat in a little alcove, smiling at the pleasure of all the people who went to and fro across the shining floor, he came and touched me, and spoke to me so that I was forced to listen. And he asked that he might speak to me for a little time apart.

"'No,' I said. 'I have no secrets from this lady. What do you want to tell me?'

"He said it was a trivial matter, or at least a dry matter, for a lady to hear.

"'Perhaps for me to hear,' said I.

"He glanced at her, as though almost he would appeal to her. Then he asked me suddenly if I had heard of a great and avenging declaration that Evesham had made. Now, Evesham had always before been the man next to myself in the leadership of that great party in the north. He was a forcible, hard and tactless man, and only I had been able to control and soften him. It was on his account even more than my own, I think, that the others had been so dismayed at my retreat. So this question about what he had done reawakened my old interest in the life I had put aside just for a moment.

"'I have taken no heed of any news for many days,' I said. 'What has Evesham been saying?'

"And with that the man began, nothing loath, and I must confess even I was struck by Evesham's reckless folly in the wild and threatening words he had used. And this messenger they had sent to me not only told me of Evesham's speech, but went on to ask counsel and to point out what need they had of me. While he talked, my lady sat a little forward and watched his face and mine.

"My old habits of scheming and organising reasserted themselves. I could even see myself suddenly returning to the north, and all the dramatic effect of it. All that this man said witnessed to the disorder of the party indeed, but not to its damage. I should go back stronger than I had come. And then I thought of my lady. You see—how can I tell you? There were certain peculiarities of our relationship—as things are I need not tell you about that—which would render her presence with me impossible. I should have had to leave her; indeed, I should have had to renounce her clearly and openly, if I was to do all that I could do in the north. And the man knew THAT, even as he talked to her and me, knew it as well as she did, that my steps to duty were—first, separation, then abandonment. At the touch of that thought my dream of a return was shattered. I turned on the man suddenly, as he was imagining his eloquence was gaining ground with me.

"'What have I to do with these things now?' I said. 'I have done with them. Do you think I am coquetting with your people in coming here?'

"'No,' he said; 'but—'

"'Why cannot you leave me alone? I have done with these things. I have ceased to be anything but a private man.'

"'Yes,' he answered. 'But have you thought?—this talk of war, these reckless challenges, these wild aggressions—'

"I stood up.

"'No,' I cried. 'I won't hear you. I took count of all those things, I weighed them—and I have come away.'

"He seemed to consider the possibility of persistence. He looked from me to where the lady sat regarding us.

"'War,' he said, as if he were speaking to himself, and then turned slowly from me and walked away. I stood, caught in the whirl of thoughts his appeal had set going.

"I heard my lady's voice.

"'Dear,' she said; 'but if they have need of you—'

"She did not finish her sentence, she let it rest there. I turned to her sweet face, and the balance of my mood swayed and reeled.

"'They want me only to do the thing they dare not do themselves,' I said. 'If they distrust Evesham they must settle with him themselves.'

"She looked at me doubtfully.

"'But war—' she said.

"I saw a doubt on her face that I had seen before, a doubt of herself and me, the first shadow of the discovery that, seen strongly and completely, must drive us apart for ever.

"Now, I was an older mind than hers, and I could sway her to this belief or that.

"'My dear one,' I said, 'you must not trouble over these things. There will be no war. Certainly there will be no war. The age of wars is past. Trust me to know the justice of this case. They have no right upon me, dearest, and no one has a right upon me. I have been free to choose my life, and I have chosen this.'

"'But WAR—' she said.

"I sat down beside her. I put an arm behind her and took her hand in mine. I set myself to drive that doubt away—I set myself to fill her mind with pleasant things again. I lied to her, and in lying to her I lied also to myself. And she was only too ready to believe me, only too ready to forget.

"Very soon the shadow had gone again, and we were hastening to our bathing-place in the Grotta del Bovo Marino, where it was our custom to bathe every day. We swam and splashed one another, and in that buoyant water I seemed to become something lighter and stronger than a man. And at last we came out dripping and rejoicing and raced among the rocks. And then I put on a dry bathing-dress, and we sat to bask in the sun, and presently I nodded, resting my head against her knee, and she put her hand upon my hair and stroked it softly and I dozed. And behold! as it were with the snapping of the string of a violin, I was awakening, and I was in my own bed in Liverpool, in the life of to-day.

"Only for a time I could not believe that all these vivid moments had been no more than the substance of a dream.

"In truth, I could not believe it a dream for all the sobering reality of things about me. I bathed and dressed as it were by habit, and as I shaved I argued why I of all men should leave the woman I loved to go back to fantastic politics in the hard and strenuous north. Even if Evesham did force the world back to war, what was that to me? I was a man, with the heart of a man, and why should I feel the responsibility of a deity for the way the world might go?

"You know that is not quite the way I think about affairs, about my real affairs. I am a solicitor, you know, with a point of view.

"The vision was so real, you must understand, so utterly unlike a dream that I kept perpetually recalling little irrelevant details; even the ornament of a book-cover that lay on my wife's sewing-machine in the breakfast-room recalled with the utmost vividness the gilt line that ran about the seat in the alcove where I had talked with the messenger from my deserted party. Have you ever heard of a dream that had a quality like that?"

"Like—?"

"So that afterwards you remembered little details you had forgotten."

I thought. I had never noticed the point before, but he was right.

"Never," I said. "That is what you never seem to do with dreams."

"No," he answered. "But that is just what I did. I am a solicitor, you must understand, in Liverpool, and I could not help wondering what the clients and business people I found myself talking to in my office would think if I told them suddenly I was in love with a girl who would be born a couple of hundred years or so hence, and worried about the politics of my great-great-

great-grandchildren. I was chiefly busy that day negotiating a ninety-nine-year building lease. It was a private builder in a hurry, and we wanted to tie him in every possible way. I had an interview with him, and he showed a certain want of temper that sent me to bed still irritated. That night I had no dream. Nor did I dream the next night, at least, to remember.

"Something of that intense reality of conviction vanished. I began to feel sure it WAS a dream. And then it came again.

"When the dream came again, nearly four days later, it was very different. I think it certain that four days had also elapsed in the dream. Many things had happened in the north, and the shadow of them was back again between us, and this time it was not so easily dispelled. I began, I know, with moody musings. Why, in spite of all, should I go back, go back for all the rest of my days to toil and stress, insults and perpetual dissatisfaction, simply to save hundreds of millions of common people, whom I did not love, whom too often I could do no other than despise, from the stress and anguish of war and infinite misrule? And after all I might fail. THEY all sought their own narrow ends, and why should not I—why should not I also live as a man? And out of such thoughts her voice summoned me, and I lifted my eyes.

"I found myself awake and walking. We had come out above the Pleasure City, we were near the summit of Monte Solaro and looking towards the bay. It was the late afternoon and very clear. Far away to the left Ischia hung in a golden haze between sea and sky, and Naples was coldly white against the hills, and before us was Vesuvius with a tall and slender streamer feathering at last towards the south, and the ruins of Torre dell' Annunziata and Castellamare glittering and near."

I interrupted suddenly: "You have been to Capri, of course?"

"Only in this dream," he said, "only in this dream. All across the bay beyond Sorrento were the floating palaces of the Pleasure City moored and chained. And northward were the broad floating stages that received the aeroplanes. Aeroplanes fell out of the sky every afternoon, each bringing its thousands of pleasure-seekers from the uttermost parts of the earth to Capri and its delights. All these things, I say, stretched below.

"But we noticed them only incidentally because of an unusual sight that evening had to show. Five war aeroplanes that had long slumbered useless in the distant arsenals of the Rhinemouth were manoeuvring now in the eastward sky. Evesham had astonished the world by producing them and others, and sending them to circle here and there. It was the threat material in the great game of bluff he was playing, and it had taken even me by surprise. He was one of those incredibly stupid energetic people who seem sent by Heaven to create disasters. His energy to the first glance seemed so wonderfully like capacity! But he had no imagination, no invention, only a stupid, vast, driving force of will, and a mad faith in his stupid idiot 'luck' to pull him through. I remember how we stood out upon the headland watching the squadron circling far away, and how I weighed the full meaning of the sight, seeing clearly the way things must go. And then even it was not too late. I might have gone back, I think, and saved the world. The people of the north would follow me, I knew, granted only that in one thing I respected their moral standards. The east and south would trust me as they would trust no other northern man. And I knew I had only to put it to her and she would have let me go.... Not because she did not love me!

"Only I did not want to go; my will was all the other way about. I had so newly thrown off the incubus of responsibility: I was still so fresh a renegade from duty that the daylight clearness of what I OUGHT to do had no power at all to touch my will. My will was to live, to gather pleasures and make my dear lady happy. But though this sense of vast neglected duties had no power to draw me, it could make me silent and preoccupied, it robbed the days I had spent of half their brightness and roused me into dark meditations in the silence of the night. And as I stood and watched Evesham's aeroplanes sweep to and fro—those birds of infinite ill omen—she stood beside me watching me, perceiving the trouble indeed, but not perceiving it clearly her eyes questioning my face, her expression shaded with perplexity. Her face was grey because the sunset was fading out of the sky. It was no fault of hers that she held me. She had asked me to go from her, and again in the night time and with tears she had asked me to go.

"At last it was the sense of her that roused me from my mood. I turned upon her suddenly and challenged her to race down the mountain slopes. 'No,' she said, as if I jarred with her gravity, but I was resolved to end that gravity, and made her run—no one can be very grey and sad who is out of breath—and when she stumbled I ran with my hand beneath her arm. We ran down past a couple of men, who turned back staring in astonishment at my behaviour—they must have recognised my face. And halfway down the slope came a tumult in the air, clang-clank, clang-clank, and we stopped, and presently over the hill-crest those war things came flying one behind the other."

The man seemed hesitating on the verge of a description.

"What were they like?" I asked.

"They had never fought," he said. "They were just like our ironclads are nowadays; they had never fought. No one knew what they might do, with excited men inside them; few even cared to speculate. They were great driving things shaped like spearheads without a shaft, with a propeller in the place of the shaft."

"Steel?"

"Not steel."

"Aluminium?"

"No, no, nothing of that sort. An alloy that was very common—as common as brass, for example. It was called—let me see—." He squeezed his forehead with the fingers of one hand. "I am forgetting everything," he said.

"And they carried guns?"

"Little guns, firing high explosive shells. They fired the guns backwards, out of the base of the leaf, so to speak, and rammed with the beak. That was the theory, you know, but they had never been fought. No one could tell exactly what was going to happen. And meanwhile I suppose it was very fine to go whirling through the air like a flight of young swallows, swift and easy. I guess the captains tried not to think too clearly what the real thing would be like. And these flying war machines, you know, were only one sort of the endless war contrivances that had been invented and had fallen into abeyance during the long peace. There were all sorts of these things that people were routing out and furbishing up; infernal things, silly things; things that had never been tried; big engines, terrible explosives, great guns. You know the silly way of these ingenious sort of men who make these things; they turn 'em out as beavers build dams, and with no more sense of the rivers they're going to divert and the lands they're going to flood!

"As we went down the winding stepway to our hotel again, in the twilight, I foresaw it all: I saw how clearly and inevitably things were driving for war in Evesham's silly, violent hands, and I had some inkling of what war was bound to be under these new conditions. And even then, though I knew it was drawing near the limit of my opportunity, I could find no will to go back."

He sighed.

"That was my last chance.

"We didn't go into the city until the sky was full of stars, so we walked out upon the high terrace, to and fro, and—she counselled me to go back.

"'My dearest,' she said, and her sweet face looked up to me, 'this is Death. This life you lead is Death. Go back to them, go back to your duty—.'

"She began to weep, saying, between her sobs, and clinging to my arm as she said it, 'Go back—Go back.'

"Then suddenly she fell mute, and, glancing down at her face, I read in an instant the thing she had thought to do. It was one of those moments when one SEES.

"'No!' I said.

"'No?' she asked, in surprise, and I think a little fearful at the answer to her thought.

"'Nothing,' I said, 'shall send me back. Nothing! I have chosen. Love, I have chosen, and the world must go. Whatever happens I will live this life—I will live for YOU! It—nothing shall turn me aside; nothing, my dear one. Even if you died—even if you died—'

"'Yes,' she murmured, softly.

"'Then—I also would die.'

"And before she could speak again I began to talk, talking eloquently—as I COULD do in that life—talking to exalt love, to make the life we were living seem heroic and glorious; and the thing I was deserting something hard and enormously ignoble that it was a fine thing to set aside. I bent all my mind to throw that glamour upon it, seeking not only to convert her but myself to that. We talked, and she clung to me, torn too between all that she deemed noble and all that she knew was sweet. And at last I did make it heroic, made all the thickening disaster of the world only a sort of glorious setting to our unparalleled love, and we two poor foolish souls strutted there at last, clad in that splendid delusion, drunken rather with that glorious delusion, under the still stars.

"And so my moment passed.

"It was my last chance. Even as we went to and fro there, the leaders of the south and east were gathering their resolve, and the hot answer that shattered Evesham's bluffing for ever, took shape and waited. And all over Asia, and the ocean, and the south, the air and the wires were throbbing with their warnings to prepare—prepare.

"No one living, you know, knew what war was; no one could imagine, with all these new inventions, what horror war might bring. I believe most people still believed it would be a matter of bright uniforms and shouting charges and triumphs and flags and bands—in a time when half the world drew its food supply from regions ten thousand miles away—."

The man with the white face paused. I glanced at him, and his face was intent on the floor of the carriage. A little railway station, a string of loaded trucks, a signal-box, and the back of a cottage, shot by the carriage window, and a bridge passed with a clap of noise, echoing the tumult of the train.

"After that," he said, "I dreamt often. For three weeks of nights that dream was my life. And the worst of it was there were nights when I could not dream, when I lay tossing on a bed in THIS accursed life; and THERE—

somewhere lost to me—things were happening—momentous, terrible things…. I lived at nights—my days, my waking days, this life I am living now, became a faded, far-away dream, a drab setting, the cover of the book."

He thought.

"I could tell you all, tell you every little thing in the dream, but as to what I did in the daytime—no. I could not tell—I do not remember. My memory—my memory has gone. The business of life slips from me—"

He leant forward, and pressed his hands upon his eyes. For a long time he said nothing.

"And then?" said I.

"The war burst like a hurricane."

He stared before him at unspeakable things.

"And then?" I urged again.

"One touch of unreality," he said, in the low tone of a man who speaks to himself, "and they would have been nightmares. But they were not nightmares—they were not nightmares. NO!"

He was silent for so long that it dawned upon me that there was a danger of losing the rest of the story. But he went on talking again in the same tone of questioning self-communion.

"What was there to do but flight? I had not thought the war would touch Capri—I had seemed to see Capri as being out of it all, as the contrast to it all; but two nights after the whole place was shouting and bawling, every woman almost and every other man wore a badge—Evesham's badge—and there was no music but a jangling war-song over and over again, and everywhere men enlisting, and in the dancing halls they were drilling. The whole island was awhirl with rumours; it was said, again and again, that fighting had begun. I had not expected this. I had seen so little of the life of pleasure that I had failed to reckon with this violence of the amateurs. And as for me, I was out of it. I was like a man who might have prevented the firing of a magazine. The time had gone. I was no one; the vainest stripling with a badge counted for more than I. The crowd jostled us and bawled in our ears; that accursed song deafened us; a woman shrieked at my lady because no badge was on her, and we two went back to our own place again, ruffled and insulted—my lady white and silent, and I aquiver with rage. So furious was I, I could have quarrelled with her if I could have found one shade of accusation in her eyes.

"All my magnificence had gone from me. I walked up and down our rock cell, and outside was the darkling sea and a light to the southward that flared and passed and came again.

"'We must get out of this place,' I said over and over. 'I have made my choice, and I will have no hand in these troubles. I will have nothing of this war. We have taken our lives out of all these things. This is no refuge for us. Let us go.'

"And the next day we were already in flight from the war that covered the world.

"And all the rest was Flight—all the rest was Flight."

He mused darkly.

"How much was there of it?"

He made no answer.

"How many days?"

His face was white and drawn and his hands were clenched. He took no heed of my curiosity.

I tried to draw him back to his story with questions.

"Where did you go?" I said.

"When?"

"When you left Capri."

"Southwest," he said, and glanced at me for a second. "We went in a boat."

"But I should have thought an aeroplane?"

"They had been seized."

I questioned him no more. Presently I thought he was beginning again. He broke out in an argumentative monotone:

"But why should it be? If, indeed, this battle, this slaughter and stress IS life, why have we this craving for pleasure and beauty? If there IS no refuge, if there is no place of peace, and if all our dreams of quiet places are a folly and a snare, why have we such dreams? Surely it was no ignoble cravings, no base intentions, had brought us to this; it was Love had isolated us. Love had come to me with her eyes and robed in her beauty, more glorious than all else in life, in the very shape and colour of life, and summoned me away. I had silenced all the voices, I had answered all the questions—I had come to her. And suddenly there was nothing but War and Death!"

I had an inspiration. "After all," I said, "it could have been only a dream."

"A dream!" he cried, flaming upon me, "a dream—when even now—"

For the first time he became animated. A faint flush crept into his cheek. He raised his open hand and clenched it, and dropped it to his knee. He spoke, looking away from me, and for all the rest of the time he looked away. "We are but phantoms," he said, "and the phantoms of phantoms, desires like cloud shadows and wills of straw that eddy in the wind; the days pass, use and wont carry us through as a train carries the shadow of its lights, so be it! But one thing is real and certain, one thing is no dreamstuff, but eternal and enduring. It is the centre of my life, and all other things about it are subordinate or altogether vain. I loved her, that woman of a dream. And she and I are dead together!

"A dream! How can it be a dream, when it drenched a living life with unappeasable sorrow, when it makes all that I have lived for and cared for, worthless and unmeaning?

"Until that very moment when she was killed I believed we had still a chance of getting away," he said. "All through the night and morning that we sailed across the sea from Capri to Salerno, we talked of escape. We were full of hope, and it clung about us to the end, hope for the life together we should lead, out of it all, out of the battle and struggle, the wild and empty passions, the empty arbitrary 'thou shalt' and 'thou shalt not' of the world. We were uplifted, as though our quest was a holy thing, as though love for one another was a mission....

"Even when from our boat we saw the fair face of that great rock Capri—already scarred and gashed by the gun emplacements and hiding-places that were to make it a fastness—we reckoned nothing of the imminent slaughter, though the fury of preparation hung about in puffs and clouds of dust at a hundred points amidst the grey; but, indeed, I made a text of that and talked. There, you know, was the rock, still beautiful, for all its scars, with its countless windows and arches and ways, tier upon tier, for a thousand feet, a vast carving of grey, broken by vine-clad terraces, and lemon and orange groves, and masses of agave and prickly pear, and puffs of almond blossom. And out under the archway that is built over the Piccola Marina other boats were coming; and as we came round the cape and within sight of the mainland, another little string of boats came into view, driving before the wind towards the southwest. In a little while a multitude had come out, the remoter just little specks of ultramarine in the shadow of the eastward cliff.

"'It is love and reason,' I said, 'fleeing from all this madness, of war.'

"And though we presently saw a squadron of aeroplanes flying across the southern sky we did not heed it. There it was—a line of little dots in the sky—and then more, dotting the southeastern horizon, and then still more, until all that quarter of the sky was stippled with blue specks. Now they were all thin little strokes of blue, and now one and now a multitude would heel and catch the sun and become short flashes of light. They came rising and falling and growing larger, like some huge flight of gulls or rooks, or such-like birds moving with a marvellous uniformity, and ever as they drew nearer they spread over a greater width of sky. The southward wing flung itself in an arrow-headed cloud athwart the sun. And then suddenly they swept round to the eastward and streamed eastward, growing smaller and smaller and clearer and clearer again until they vanished from the sky. And after that we noted to the northward and very high Evesham's fighting machines hanging high over Naples like an evening swarm of gnats.

"It seemed to have no more to do with us than a flight of birds.

"Even the mutter of guns far away in the southeast seemed to us to signify nothing....

"Each day, each dream after that, we were still exalted, still seeking that refuge where we might live and love. Fatigue had come upon us, pain and many distresses. For though we were dusty and stained by our toilsome tramping, and half starved and with the horror of the dead men we had seen and the flight of the peasants—for very soon a gust of fighting swept up the peninsula—with these things haunting our minds it still resulted only in a deepening resolution to escape. O, but she was brave and patient! She who had never faced hardship and exposure had courage for herself—and me. We went to and fro seeking an outlet, over a country all commandeered and ransacked by the gathering hosts of war. Always we went on foot. At first there were other fugitives, but we did not mingle with them. Some escaped northward, some were caught in the torrent of peasantry that swept along the main roads; many gave themselves into the hands of the soldiery and were sent northward. Many of the men were impressed. But we kept away from these things; we had brought no money to bribe a passage north, and I feared for my lady at the hands of these conscript crowds. We had landed at Salerno, and we had been turned back from Cava, and we had tried to cross towards Taranto by a pass over Mount Alburno, but we had been driven back for want of food, and so we had come down among the marshes by Paestum, where those great temples stand alone. I had some vague idea that by Paestum it might be possible to find a boat or something, and take once more to sea. And there it was the battle overtook us.

"A sort of soul-blindness had me. Plainly I could see that we were being hemmed in; that the great net of that giant Warfare had us in its toils. Many times we had seen the levies that had come down from the north going to and fro, and had come upon them in the distance amidst the mountains making ways for the ammunition and preparing the mounting of the guns. Once we fancied they had fired at us, taking us for spies—at any rate a shot had gone shuddering over us. Several times we had hidden in woods from hovering aeroplanes.

"But all these things do not matter now, these nights of flight and pain.... We were in an open place near those great temples at Paestum, at last, on a blank stony place dotted with spiky bushes, empty and desolate and so flat that a grove of eucalyptus far away showed to the feet of its stems. How I can see it! My lady was sitting down under a bush, resting a little, for she was very weak and weary, and I was standing up watching to see if I could tell the distance of the firing that came and went. They were still, you know, fighting far from each other, with those terrible new weapons that had never before been used: guns that would carry beyond sight, and aeroplanes that would do—What THEY would do no man could foretell.

"I knew that we were between the two armies, and that they drew together. I knew we were in danger, and that we could not stop there and rest!

"Though all these things were in my mind, they were in the background. They seemed to be affairs beyond our concern. Chiefly, I was thinking of my lady. An aching distress filled me. For the first time she had owned herself beaten and had fallen a-weeping. Behind me I could hear her sobbing, but I would not turn round to her because I knew she had need of weeping, and had held herself so far and so long for me. It was well, I thought, that she would weep and rest and then we would toil on again, for I had no inkling of the thing that hung so near. Even now I can see her as she sat there, her lovely hair upon her shoulder, can mark again the deepening hollow of her cheek.

"'If we had parted,' she said, 'if I had let you go.'

"'No,' said I. 'Even now, I do not repent. I will not repent; I made my choice, and I will hold on to the end."

"And then—

"Overhead in the sky something flashed and burst, and all about us I heard the bullets making a noise like a handful of peas suddenly thrown. They chipped the stones about us, and whirled fragments from the bricks and passed...."

He put his hand to his mouth, and then moistened his lips.

"At the flash I had turned about....

"You know—she stood up—

"She stood up; you know, and moved a step towards me—

"As though she wanted to reach me—

"And she had been shot through the heart."

He stopped and stared at me. I felt all that foolish incapacity an Englishman feels on such occasions. I met his eyes for a moment, and then stared out of the window. For a long space we kept silence. When at last I looked at him he was sitting back in his corner, his arms folded, and his teeth gnawing at his knuckles.

He bit his nail suddenly, and stared at it.

"I carried her," he said, "towards the temples, in my arms—as though it mattered. I don't know why. They seemed a sort of sanctuary, you know, they had lasted so long, I suppose.

"She must have died almost instantly. Only—I talked to her—all the way."

Silence again.

"I have seen those temples," I said abruptly, and indeed he had brought those still, sunlit arcades of worn sandstone very vividly before me.

"It was the brown one, the big brown one. I sat down on a fallen pillar and held her in my arms.... Silent after the first babble was over. And after a little while the lizards came out and ran about again, as though nothing unusual was going on, as though nothing had changed.... It was tremendously still there, the sun high, and the shadows still; even the shadows of the weeds upon the entablature were still—in spite of the thudding and banging that went all about the sky.

"I seem to remember that the aeroplanes came up out of the south, and that the battle went away to the west. One aeroplane was struck, and overset and fell. I remember that—though it didn't interest me in the least. It didn't seem to signify. It was like a wounded gull, you know—flapping for a time in the water. I could see it down the aisle of the temple—a black thing in the bright blue water.

"Three or four times shells burst about the beach, and then that ceased. Each time that happened all the lizards scuttled in and hid for a space. That was all the mischief done, except that once a stray bullet gashed the stone hard by—made just a fresh bright surface.

"As the shadows grew longer, the stillness seemed greater.

"The curious thing," he remarked, with the manner of a man who makes a trivial conversation, "is that I didn't THINK—I didn't think at all. I sat with her in my arms amidst the stones—in a sort of lethargy—stagnant.

"And I don't remember waking up. I don't remember dressing that day. I know I found myself in my office, with my letters all slit open in front of me, and how I was struck by the absurdity of being there, seeing that in reality I was sitting, stunned, in that Paestum temple with a dead woman in my arms. I read my letters like a machine. I have forgotten what they were about."

He stopped, and there was a long silence.

Suddenly I perceived that we were running down the incline from Chalk Farm to Euston. I started at this passing of time. I turned on him with a brutal question, with the tone of Now or never.

"And did you dream again?"

"Yes."

He seemed to force himself to finish. His voice was very low.

"Once more, and as it were only for a few instants. I seemed to have suddenly awakened out of a great apathy, to have risen into a sitting position, and the body lay there on the stones beside me. A gaunt body. Not her, you know. So soon—it was not her....

"I may have heard voices. I do not know. Only I knew clearly that men were coming into the solitude and that that was a last outrage.

"I stood up and walked through the temple, and then there came into sight— first one man with a yellow face, dressed in a uniform of dirty white, trimmed with blue, and then several, climbing to the crest of the old wall of the vanished city, and crouching there. They were little bright figures in the sunlight, and there they hung, weapon in hand, peering cautiously before them.

"And further away I saw others and then more at another point in the wall. It was a long lax line of men in open order.

"Presently the man I had first seen stood up and shouted a command, and his men came tumbling down the wall and into the high weeds towards the temple. He scrambled down with them and led them. He came facing towards me, and when he saw me he stopped.

"At first I had watched these men with a mere curiosity, but when I had seen they meant to come to the temple I was moved to forbid them. I shouted to the officer.

"'You must not come here,' I cried, '*I* am here. I am here with my dead.'

"He stared, and then shouted a question back to me in some unknown tongue.

"I repeated what I had said.

"He shouted again, and I folded my arms and stood still. Presently he spoke to his men and came forward. He carried a drawn sword.

"I signed to him to keep away, but he continued to advance. I told him again very patiently and clearly: 'You must not come here. These are old temples and I am here with my dead.'

"Presently he was so close I could see his face clearly. It was a narrow face, with dull grey eyes, and a black moustache. He had a scar on his upper lip, and he was dirty and unshaven. He kept shouting unintelligible things, questions perhaps, at me.

"I know now that he was afraid of me, but at the time that did not occur to me. As I tried to explain to him he interrupted me in imperious tones, bidding me, I suppose, stand aside.

"He made to go past me, And I caught hold of him.

"I saw his face change at my grip.

"'You fool,' I cried. 'Don't you know? She is dead!'

"He started back. He looked at me with cruel eyes. I saw a sort of exultant resolve leap into them—delight. Then, suddenly, with a scowl, he swept his sword back—SO—and thrust."

He stopped abruptly. I became aware of a change in the rhythm of the train. The brakes lifted their voices and the carriage jarred and jerked. This present world insisted upon itself, became clamorous. I saw through the steamy window huge electric lights glaring down from tall masts upon a fog, saw rows of stationary empty carriages passing by, and then a signal-box, hoisting its constellation of green and red into the murky London twilight marched after them. I looked again at his drawn features.

"He ran me through the heart. It was with a sort of astonishment—no fear, no pain—but just amazement, that I felt it pierce me, felt the sword drive home into my body. It didn't hurt, you know. It didn't hurt at all."

The yellow platform lights came into the field of view, passing first rapidly, then slowly, and at last stopping with a jerk. Dim shapes of men passed to and fro without.

"Euston!" cried a voice.

"Do you mean—?"

"There was no pain, no sting or smart. Amazement and then darkness sweeping over everything. The hot, brutal face before me, the face of the man who had killed me, seemed to recede. It swept out of existence—"

"Euston!" clamoured the voices outside; "Euston!"

The carriage door opened, admitting a flood of sound, and a porter stood regarding us. The sounds of doors slamming, and the hoof-clatter of cab-horses, and behind these things the featureless remote roar of the London cobble-stones, came to my ears. A truckload of lighted lamps blazed along the platform.

"A darkness, a flood of darkness that opened and spread and blotted out all things."

"Any luggage, sir?" said the porter.

"And that was the end?" I asked.

He seemed to hesitate. Then, almost inaudibly, he answered, "No."

"You mean?"

"I couldn't get to her. She was there on the other side of the Temple—And then—"

"Yes," I insisted. "Yes?"

"Nightmares," he cried; "nightmares indeed! My God! Great birds that fought and tore."

Milton Keynes UK
Ingram Content Group UK Ltd.
UKHW042145281024
450365UK00010B/621